Continuing Professional Development in Social Work

LYNNE RUTTER

Series Editor: Keith Brown

SAGE | LearningMatters

Los Angeles | London | New Delhi
Singapore | Washington DC

Learning Matters
An imprint of SAGE Publications Ltd
1 Oliver's Yard
55 City Road
London EC1Y 1SP

SAGE Publications Inc.
2455 Teller Road
Thousand Oaks, California 91320

SAGE Publications India Pvt Ltd
B 1/I 1 Mohan Cooperative Industrial Area
Mathura Road
New Delhi 110 044

SAGE Publications Asia-Pacific Pte Ltd
3 Church Street
#10-04 Samsung Hub
Singapore 049483

Editor: Luke Block
Development editor: Lauren Simpson
Production controller: Chris Marke
Project management: Swales & Willis Ltd, Exeter,
Devon
Marketing manager: Tamara Navaratnam
Cover design: Wendy Scott
Typeset by: Swales & Willis Ltd, Exeter, Devon
Printed by: MPG Books Group, Bodmin, Cornwall

Library of Congress Control Number: 2012945182

British Library Cataloguing in Publication Data

A catalogue record for this book is available from the
British Library

ISBN 978 1 44626 656 4
ISBN 978 1 44626 657 1 (pbk)

MIX
Paper from
responsible sources
FSC® C018575
www.fsc.org

Contents

List of illustrations and activities

List of figures

List of tables

List of activities

Foreword

Ongoing education, learning and training are vital to both personal and workforce development and should be a collaborative venture between practitioners, employers and providers. However, there is a shift from looking at continuing professional development (CPD) as something that is foisted upon staff towards seeing it as a more proactive process dependent on individual commitment, responsibility and engagement. Recent social work CPD initiatives (e.g. the Professional Capabilities Framework) encourage practitioners to become engaged in identifying their professional learning needs and to commit to the time needed to meet them in a systematic way.

This book aims to support this process by helping social workers understand their professional development, the level and style of learning required in the workplace, and to ensure CPD activities meet individual, organisational and professional requirements. It supports the view that ongoing professional learning should be engaged with at an appropriate level (i.e. one associated with complex thinking and practices) and approached holistically so that the resulting development of professional reasoning and judgement can be appropriately recognised and evaluated. The systematic planning, recording, assessing, evaluating and/or accreditation of CPD is now an important consideration in determining the level of learning that has occurred and the impact it has had on the individual, their professional practice and the service.

This book also enhances the principles of lifelong learning and develops the use of tools such as critical thinking and reflection, enabling practitioners to plan, undertake and articulate meaningful professional development. Moreover, the content within:

- enables practitioners to take responsibility for ongoing learning and planning, undertaking and evaluating their professional development;

- links to the social work CPD framework, the Professional Capabilities Framework and Health and Care Professions Council (HCPC) re-registration requirements;

- works to Munro (2011) recommendations by acknowledging and exploring professional judgement and learning cultures.

As is always the case in this series, this text is written and designed to support the development of the best possible social work practice, in order that vulnerable citizens in society, whoever and wherever they are, can be assured of receiving a professional social work service which is valued, effective and truly makes a difference to their lives.

Professor Keith Brown
Director of the Centre for Post-Qualifying Social Work
Bournemouth University

About the author

Lynne Rutter holds academic and professional qualifications in education and has several years' experience of developing and delivering Bournemouth University programmes. Her doctorate research focused on the development of professional knowledge and she is a co-author of the Sage/Learning Matters texts *Critical Thinking and Professional Judgement for Social Work* and *The Practice Educator's Handbook*. Currently she is developing continuing professional development units for post-qualifying social work.

Introduction

Social work as a profession has been experiencing a significant period of change over recent years. Work by the Social Work Reform Board (SWRB) and The College of Social Work (referred to as The College hereafter) is helping to turn recommendations made by the Social Work Task Force (SWTF, 2009) into ideas which will be of practical help on the ground, and ensure sustainable improvements to services for children, adults and families. Within this agenda is a growing appreciation of the uncertain and complex situations that social workers have to deal with. The SWRB (2010, 2011) and the Munro Review of Child Protection (Munro, 2011) have stressed the need to move towards a more creative and flexible approach to service provision in order to take account of this complexity, and for social workers to have more freedom to exercise their professional judgement.

In this environment, continuing professional development (CPD) has to acknowledge and involve the processes of professional reasoning and judgement, the complexity and uncertainty of social work practice, the relational nature of policy and procedure, as well as a range of social and political influences. This means that it goes beyond a requirement to passively update skills and knowledge; it becomes an individual responsibility to actively make sense of ongoing learning and build expertise in its widest sense. CPD is a crucial and challenging component of professional practice and also a very personal and meaningful one.

In this Introduction we will start to identify a number of features associated with CPD for social work today, the approach taken to CPD and also some fundamental concerns associated with it too. First, we will explore what the book is aiming to do.

The purpose of this book

The primary purpose of this book is to assist post-qualifying social workers in England who are undertaking CPD within the new frameworks set out by the SWRB (2011) and The College (**www.collegeofsocialwork.org**). The book is useful for those undertaking managerial or leadership roles but it has been written for all practitioners who have completed their first assessed year in practice and are continuing to develop their expertise. Many of the ideas contained in this book should also prove useful and relevant for professionals working in associated fields, such as care managers and health workers, across all parts of the UK. For newly qualified social work practitioners who are undertaking their assessed first year, specialist advice is provided in an accompanying text in this series by Keen et al. (2012) – *Newly Qualified Social Workers: A Practice Guide to the Assessed and Supported Year in Employment*, 2nd edition.

This book takes a wide view of the subject of CPD and explores and explains a range of ideas associated with professional practice and work-based learning, some of which can be found in other books written with my colleagues (e.g. Williams and Rutter, 2010; Rutter and Brown, 2011; Brown et al., 2012; Williams et al., 2012). These ideas have been brought together and can be used as a starting point from which to understand and also undertake systematic and in-depth learning and development. This learning and development is also guided and supported by a number of suggested approaches and processes. The evidencing of learning and its outcomes for more formalised CPD processes is also considered. Throughout, the book blends practical information and advice with material aimed at developing an understanding of key concepts and ideas which will encourage you to think about CPD in a personal and also a wider sense. The book will not provide you with a defined process or a prescriptive list of things to do, but it can help you to develop and follow a CPD pathway which best suits your particular needs and style. For managers and leaders, it can also help with understanding the CPD needs of others, both strategically and in providing more practical support.

CPD for social work today

There are a number of key drivers and initiatives which strongly influence the nature of CPD at the present time. They include:

- the new CPD framework;

- the Professional Capabilities Framework;

- an outcomes-based approach to CPD.

The new CPD framework, developed by The College, provides structure and support for social workers to progress throughout their careers; it replaces the Post-Qualifying (PQ) Framework. It recognises the wide range of CPD activities such as work-based training, academic courses and informal learning such as case discussions, joint working, personal research and project work. The central mechanism is the Professional Capabilities Framework or PCF (**www.collegeof socialwork.org/pcf.aspx**), which sets national and professional standards for all levels from entry through to principal social worker roles. The PCF aims to encourage the articulation and assessment of learning and development occurring within both educational and practice settings. The PCF replaces the National Occupational Standards and is also expected to be used in conjunction with the Standards for Employers and Supervision Framework, held by the Local Government Association (**www.education.gov.uk/swrb/employers**).

The Health and Care Professions Council (HCPC) (**www.hcpc-uk.org**) has superseded the General Social Care Council (GSCC) as the body for professional registration and standards to ensure safe and effective practice for social workers in England. The HCPC provides a range of guidance about CPD responsibilities via its website. Professional re-registration for social workers now becomes obligatory after two years, and is based on self-evaluation, outcomes and a portfolio of evidence of learning (see Appendix 1 for more information). It means that it is now the output of learning that is taken into account for CPD, rather than input such as a defined numbers of days or hours. This is a significant shift in the type of approach being required for CPD in respect of re-registration and will be explored in more detail later.

At the time of writing, The College is developing an online portfolio for its members for the planning and recording of CPD activity which relates to the PCF, so that individual learning plans can be developed within the context of career development and progression. The online portfolio will also enable direct downloading of information and evidence to the HCPC template for re-registration.

HCPC guidance and the overall structure and intentions of the PCF will be referred to in general terms throughout. However, this book is not intended to provide detailed instructions because each of you will be following a unique path which you need to work out for yourselves. The advice is to refer regularly to the resources and guidance contained on The College and the HCPC websites, which are likely to be modified and developed over time.

Key approaches

Self-managed learning

In general, the new CPD agenda for social work places responsibility for professional development largely with the individual practitioner. The College explains that it is practitioners who will need to decide, together with their manager or supervisor (usually in appraisal or supervision) what their learning and personal development needs are and how they can be met. In response, this book offers an approach aligned to this new model of planning and recording CPD – one based on the principles of self-managed lifelong learning, on output, and a deliberate move away from seeing CPD as something which is dictated by others.

> *An outcomes-based approach places more responsibility on the individual to ascertain their CPD needs and evaluate the learning, demonstrating how this has improved their professional performance.*

> (O'Sullivan, 2006: 5)

Self-managed learning involves the ability to understand our personal approaches (including ideas and beliefs) towards knowledge and learning, to have a range of appropriate techniques and methods, and to be able to seek help and advice when necessary. More importantly, it involves an ability to evaluate and assess what we do against particular requirements or criteria, to recognise gaps and to persevere! Although it can seem onerous at times, an underlying key principle is to view ongoing learning as an investment in ourselves and our future, and ensure it is worthwhile to us.

CPD, whether it is undertaken within an academic environment or not, requires the disposition and skills for approaching ideas and practice analytically (being able to see the significance and importance of particular aspects), critically (being able to challenge and question), and in an evaluative way (being able to appraise and make a judgement). These key attributes will be considered throughout the book. Advice and guidance will be offered to help you assess your ability in these areas and take appropriate action to improve and develop where necessary.

Outcomes approach

Obviously, the overriding purpose of CPD is to enhance practice and service quality. Therefore, an outcomes-based approach is being promoted by the new agenda in order to take proper account of the effects of learning. In other words, CPD activity will require practitioners to demonstrate how this learning has made a difference to their practice. This includes striving for excellence in performance and service quality, adherence to a moral and ethical code of practice, being accountable, empowering others and having an awareness of the limitations and scope of practice.

It also involves the ability to express and present this output rationally and coherently for any measurement or assessment purpose, such as for appraisal, re-registration, career progression or for a formal programme. Placing the emphasis on the productivity of learning, rather than just the amount or type of learning which has been undertaken, is a very positive step towards encouraging a much fuller engagement with development opportunities. Even with all the will in the world, we are unlikely to get the best value from any learning unless something allows us, and perhaps pushes us, to put it into use and review what happens. In fact, by focusing on concrete changes in work processes or outcomes, we not only use the learning more effectively and become aware of how it is making a difference, we also become more aware of our learning processes – by realising what was learned, we can see how it was learned (Simons and Ruijters, 2001).

Unfortunately, detailing the outcomes of learning is always a *challenge* (O'Sullivan, 2006: 5) because terms like 'outcomes', 'practice' and 'service quality' will mean different things in different places and times, and for different people too. Nevertheless, we can still try to understand these terms in a way that will help us to explore, explain and articulate our learning and its impact within our particular circumstances, and also help to locate what we do in a wider context too.

Eraut (1994) notes that practice is concerned with two key interlinked areas:

1. The scope of the work being undertaken, i.e. what is done – the roles, tasks, methods, processes and procedures.

2. The quality of the work, i.e. how well it is done. This can include aspects such as 'ensuring safety and efficacy of practice; thinking critically about what is done, and how and why it is done that way; interacting well with others; acting, influencing and responding appropriately in various contexts' (O'Sullivan, 2006: 8–9).

These two areas of practice are useful distinctions and will be referred to in many of the chapters. Detailing the effect learning has within the first area noted above can be relatively simple because such things as key tasks and processes can usually be clearly designated and defined. The second area is necessarily more problematic because it requires a certain amount of creative and adaptive thinking to identify, describe and appraise the particular thinking, behaviours and attributes which are associated with quality, and which are dependent on situations and circumstances. This particular issue will occur throughout the book.

Fundamental concerns

There are a number of other underlying and unresolved dilemmas and issues associated with CPD which need to be noted at this early stage, and which also appear throughout the book.

- Being professional involves practising autonomously but also accountably. However, the balance between the two can be almost impossible to define because, again, it will vary for different situations, roles, teams, client groups and organisations, and be in contention for many.

- Although there is a need to identify the areas of practice which can be standardised and measured, it is also necessary to recognise that there are others that cannot be standardised and measured in the same way, if at all (Dunne, 2011). However, this difference does not always appear to have been taken into consideration, or even understood within some CPD arenas. Many standards and criteria, especially for the assessment of learning, have become either vague or overly prescriptive in their attempts to cover the more holistic and qualitative areas of practice because they do not recognise this difference (Potter and East, 2000). As a result, they lose or devalue the real essence of whatever it is they wish to acknowledge.

- The issue of human fallibility is extremely relevant here. People will make mistakes and all the standards, set procedures and criteria in the world will not stop this from happening. However, some organisations and governments appear to believe that having a strict adherence to set procedures will produce an absolute type of 'certainty' in practice and stop mistakes. In some areas this may be true, and in the right place it is not necessarily a bad thing; it can be essential, of course, to protect the users of services and the profession itself (Williams et al., 2012). On the other hand, this style of management can produce a heavily bureaucratised and ineffective system which actually creates obstacles to good practice by prioritising the demands of performance management over service users' needs (Munro, 2011). As Munro (20) explains further, any perceived notion of certainty and security, or a 'defence' brought about by following correct procedures, is actually false, as it 'creates a feedback loop that reinforces the defensive routine based on a procedural perspective which hampers professional learning' and stifles the development of expertise. Recognition of where strict procedure is not appropriate, and an allowance of the right balance between professional discretion and accountability (and support for it), can be difficult and elusive ideals.

- For people to learn how to make sound judgements, they need explicit recognition and support from the complete learning process, which includes this element of fallibility, rather than procedures which ignore or negate it. Otherwise, as Dunne (2011: 17) says, you may end up with a rather meaningless 'practitioner-proof mode of practice'. It is through experiences of discomfort or 'getting it wrong' that professional wisdom can grow – 'the knowing that resides in wisdom is largely a knowing that we do not know' (25). This crucial part of learning and development is not always acknowledged when CPD processes are superficial or where they focus purely on achievement; that is, when they are not sensitive enough to the idea of considering means as well as ends.

These dilemmas may not be resolvable but their influence requires an acknowledgement and where possible an effort to take account of them.

The layout of this book

This book is best read from start to finish as a number of ideas are developed throughout, but it can also be dipped into to pick up on specific topics. Chapter 1 introduces a number of general ideas associated with the notion of professional capability and expertise, which clarify the overall approach being adopted here. They help you to define what being a professional means to you, an important starting point to make CPD a meaningful endeavour. The following three chapters aim to set CPD within an appropriate learning framework so that you can undertake it as systematically as necessary, and underpin it with clear relevant learning objectives, the right approaches to learning and with appropriate levels of reflection. Chapter 5 then explores the most appropriate learning environments for CPD and the various roles other people may take in enhancing your learning. Chapter 6 aims to make CPD output clearer, and explores the PCF and a range of other frameworks that can be used to help determine progression. Chapter 7 discusses the use and accreditation of CPD learning in academic environments and also shows how CPD evidence can be created from work-based learning for a formal programme, using a specific example. Chapter 8 takes this a step further to look at expressing CPD in written form.

My hope is that by reading this material, undertaking the activities and thinking through some of these ideas, your continuing professional development (and that of anyone you are supporting, managing or leading) is meaningful and productive.

Chapter 1
Understanding CPD

In this first chapter, the term 'continuing professional development' is explored in order to create an understanding that can help make it relevant and meaningful for you. Recent ideas concerning the notion of professionalism, such as capability and judgement, will be considered in some detail first. They can help define what being a professional means to you on an individual level, helping to provide the motivation and will to learn.

What do we mean by the term 'professional'?

It could be said that social work and many of its associated professions have to operate within strict legislation, policy and procedures. This gives a framework to work within, but no matter how well defined or detailed they are, any rules or guidance still need to be managed, interpreted and implemented in real situations. Professionalism in this sense can be regarded as a high level skill consisting of a perceptive awareness of any situation and wise moral judgement in respect of it, which also draws on a range of skills and knowledge at a practical level. It is about knowing what to do, when to do it and how to do it, but also why it should be done in a certain way for a particular set of circumstances.

The professional element in practice is said to concern the thoughts, ideas, reasoning, feelings and actions involved in these judgements and decisions about what to do and when. Dalgleish (2000, cited in Collins and Daly, 2011: 20) explains that 'judgements are the inferences drawn from information, and decisions are the actions taken on the basis of these judgements'. Professionalism can therefore be seen as a process or a 'quality of judgement' (5).

Munro (2011) also recognises that social workers need to be able to exercise judgement in their practice, rather than relying on – or being pushed into completing – set procedures, or using tools which may undermine such judgement. She says there is a need to move:

> from a system that has become over-bureaucratised and focused on compliance to one that values and develops professional expertise and is focused on the safety and welfare of children and young people.
>
> (2011: 6)

Professional judgement is associated with accountable decision-making as well as risk assessment and management, and therefore with the ability to predict the future and manage risk of harm. As Munro also highlights, there has to be a realistic expectation of professionals' ability to do this. As noted in the Introduction, such decisions are, and always will be, fallible, because human beings are essentially unpredictable – we cannot eradicate risk, only reduce the probability of harm. Any professional judgement process has to be based on realistic conceptions of human strengths and weaknesses, has to work with uncertainty and be as sound and robust as it can be. One way to manage this is to ensure the process is not only value-based but also subject to critical thinking and evaluation. This, in turn, should avoid a prescriptive approach to practice and focus on professional learning and increasing capability and expertise.

Capability

This notion of capability can be explored further to try to recognise its particular features, and allow a more explicit understanding of what it is you are developing as your practice progresses. The development of such capability should allow you to accept and deal with individual and ever-changing situations in a creative and critical way, rather than following routine and prescription practice unthinkingly.

The PCF explicitly utilises the term 'capability' in order to highlight a distinct move from the idea of 'competence', reflecting The College's aim for social work education to consider professional development in a more rounded and holistic way. We can focus our thoughts on the difference between 'capability' and 'competence' by studying Table 1.1, and considering why capability is so important at a professional level.

The individual wisdom and expertise contained within this idea of professional capability seems to be embedded within our thinking and practical activity, and will be evident within the values and outcomes of practice. This means that, although there may be certain principles which need to be embedded within that practice, they will be enacted in a number of ways depending on situational and personal characteristics. This is the wisdom, if you like, which has to be developed and honed in order to ensure the process is sound. This understanding and definition of capability acknowledges the flexible, responsive, critical thinking and the moral reasoning underpinning judgement which is at the heart of professional practice dealing with risk and uncertainty and with non-routine and complex situations.

In Williams and Rutter (2010) we go further, to suggest that practice education should start from a capability approach rather than a competency-based one, because they are so fundamentally different. It could be thought that competence is the first stage before capability, because it provides the necessary foundational level of understanding and skill. Of course there has to be an underpinning knowledge, skills and value base from which to develop practice, but we argue that it should be learnt within the same approach necessary to develop future practice and not an opposing one; otherwise inappropriate and limited ways of thinking can become too embedded.

In our experience, when students have become limited by a competency-based approach, their CPD has first and foremost to become a journey towards more critical and flexible thinking. It can be very difficult to make the shift from the type and level of thinking on the left-hand section of the table to the right; it would be much more appropriate to develop the right-hand style of thinking in practitioners from the outset. Of course, this would rely on a very special type of learning environment and partnership between educators and learners which can develop foundational knowledge, skills and confidence within a framework acknowledging uncertainty and complexity. For more detail on this, please refer to Williams and Rutter (2010).

Table 1.1 Key features and thinking associated with competence and professional capability

Competence	Professional capability
Enables a professional to develop a foundational set of practical skills, knowledge and understanding of values to function well in straightforward, routine situations.	Enables a professional to develop the cognitive and affective abilities to think independently, critically and creatively in dynamic, ill-structured and unpredictable situations.
Focuses on specific procedures and roles.	Focuses on critical practice.
Is driven more by targets/assessment tasks and criteria only: reductionist view.	Is driven more by requirements for development and independent learning: holistic view.
Sees knowledge as a product. Knowledge given and received mostly unchanged and unchallenged.	Sees knowledge as a process (reason and judgement). An interpretive ability to interrogate knowledge and develop own insights.
Adopts routine thinking following set guidelines and procedures.	Adopts analytical and evaluative thinking developing professional judgement.
Can develop reliance on others or procedure.	Develops reliance on self and own judgement.
Produces easily assessed, measurable skills or knowledge-based outputs.	Produces less easily assessed or measurable cognitive-based outputs or tacit understanding.
Is more aligned with fixed thinking, unable or unwillingness to change or adapt.	Is more aligned with proactive and perceptive thinking; able and willing to change or adapt.
Encompasses nominal self-awareness; professional superiority.	Encompasses critical self-awareness; professional humility.
Likened to a cook working to recipes.	Likened to a chef – having a more complex understanding to develop own recipes.
Likened to a map reader.	Likened to a map maker.
Is based on a technocratic or technical-rational model which involves uncritical, mechanistic application of knowledge and the reduction and over-simplification of complexity, uncertainty and contingency.	Is based on a post-technocratic model which involves critically reflective interpretation and use of knowledge; appreciates and creatively takes account of situational difference and complexity, uncertainty and contingency.

Professional judgement

So, the essence of professional capability is about making unique best judgements for specific complex situations, and this requires a range of strategies, attributes and abilities. We can start to explore the idea of judgement in more detail, and an important consideration has already been mentioned in the Introduction. Attempts to specify or standardise particular processes and principles associated with professional judgement will probably not be able to fully 'capture' the diverse but also interconnected elements at play. For example, professional judgement would include an ability to evaluate evidence, to appraise situations and circumstances in order to draw sound conclusions (Collins and Daly, 2011). We could also say that the essential quality of this practice would be seen in how and why any evidence is evaluated, such as whether any type of knowledge or information is privileged or not; when and how a situation is appraised; and whether a 'sound' conclusion has been defined in the first place. These are the aspects that are less easy to capture, are associated with moral values, and may vary in differing circumstances and with different individuals. This will have implications for the assessment and evaluation of practice, dealt with in Chapter 6.

Nevertheless, making an effort to uncover, explore and understand some of the elusive aspects of professional judgement increases the possibility of becoming more aware of them in action, critically reflecting on them afterwards, and developing them more meaningfully. This can be achieved not just for your learning but also for reasons of accountability and for you to be able to share such knowledge and understanding with colleagues. Here we will explore two aspects of professional judgement: the first is practical reasoning, the second the use of knowledge.

Practical reasoning

Reasoning can be seen as a pivotal element in making inferences, judgements and decisions, whether they are about people or situations or implementing policy and legislation. It is important to acknowledge this as a cognitive process, no matter how tacit it may become in real situations, because it is the vital 'agency' or intervention of the practitioner. Practice is not just about what you are 'doing', it is very much about your thinking and reasoning underpinning that doing.

But what type of reasoning is it that we are dealing with here? We need to explore this briefly with the theory. The main point that seems relevant was mentioned earlier – professional judgements and decisions are made in respect of particular situations and outcomes. We do something in a certain way because we have considered what the situation is about and what it requires. There is a dialogue, that is, a questioning and answering aimed at understanding and achieving something, which can take both a personal and a general view of that situation (Kondrat, 1992). The dialogue concerns what to do and how best to go about it by considering ideas and options in respect of what is being seen, heard, felt and understood about the situation. As Munro (2011: 93) explains, the situation itself *talks back* to you. If a member of your staff is feeling particularly vulnerable because of organisational restructuring then your deliberation about the best way to manage their performance would not only consider your existing knowledge about anxiety and its effect on people, but also this person's particular behaviour and reactions, e.g. anger, defensiveness, bravado.

This type of dialogue can be seen to be characteristic of something called practical reasoning (Lucas, 1994). Practical reasoning is reason directed towards action, determining how to work out what to do and how to do it, and it concludes with a belief about what one ought to do: an intention or an action (Streumer, 2009). Kundin (2010) says this is the logic used in decision-making when assessing problems, analysing situations, developing questions and negotiating processes.

Fenstermacher (1994) says that practical reasoning of this sort aligns with Aristotle's notion of phronēsis, a type of reflection which deliberates between means and ends; but he also argues that it can provide the necessary justification or warrant for doing something. This is a different type of logic to that seen in academic or purely theoretical reasoning, and it is also different to an instrumental or technical type of reasoning (Rutter and Brown, 2011). Neither of these align with the active and critically reflective relationship between thought and action necessary for professional practice, seen earlier when we explored the notion of capability. Technical or instrumental reasoning only concerns itself with choosing set answers to set problems, and theoretical reasoning is concerned with finding truth through logic and considered thought. In contrast, Kemmis (1985) shows that practical reasoning considers what will be right and appropriate for a situation, and how to act in the situation as a moral question. It considers both means and ends, and allows for complexity by recognising that:

> choices need to be made about the criteria by which to judge the action to be taken (and where there may be competing criteria by which to judge it).

> (1985: 141)

Such practical reasoning and logic is, indeed, said to be a key part of professional independent judgement-making (Kondrat, 1992; Beckett and Hager, 2002), and so the overall point is that a practical reasoning process appears to lie at the heart of professional practice. It provides an appropriate approach for theory–practice integration, a more explicit focus for reflection, an output of understanding and further knowledge, and it aligns well with the notion of capability offered at the beginning of the chapter (Rutter, 2012).

One fundamental feature of practical reasoning to take into account, though, is that there is no established process to it. Any 'rules' tend to be set by the situation itself rather than imposed upon it. As seen earlier, it evolves within a context (Kondrat, 1992) and so it cannot be viewed or approached as a prescriptive list to be followed. If we impose set methods or rules for it, it will become mechanistic and meaningless. The fact that there is no set process to practical reasoning is seen as characteristic of the way experts practise in real life. The rules of decision-making are hidden and intuitive, or tacit, even for the experts themselves. As Ropo (2004: 163) explains, experts can appear *irrational*. Nevertheless, a person is an expert because he or she seems to understand the requirements of the situation better and is able to fit personal decisions, actions and interactions into the context – all fundamental aspects of practical reasoning. So, in response, we can only say that practical reasoning involves a number of fundamental aspects or key principles, as follows:

- A clear purpose and intentions.

- Relevance and sensitivity shown to the context and situation, i.e. an appreciation of what is 'right and good' for this situation based on its specific needs, complexity and uncertainty.

- Explicit and sound moral judgement.

- Use of values in deliberating between means and ends.

- Understanding, interpretation and activation of relevant knowledge, skills and values.

- A critically reflective position, e.g. consideration of alternatives.

- Use of attributes such as critical questioning, perception, discernment, insight, flexibility.

- Evaluation of progress and outcomes.

What you can do, though, is to employ this list to help acknowledge, understand and critically reflect on reasoning and judgement processes in more detail, and use that to develop practice, whether in supervision, appraisal, using the PCF or other developmental frameworks. It should help clarify and explore practice by providing a list of what 'good' practical reasoning consists of. It can be used to help direct the questioning of a piece of work and start to specify the learning, such as:

'Was I able to consider any alternatives to my initial choice of action at the time? . . . Well no, there was a lack of time to do this . . . Is there a way I can plan some time to consider them now though?'

'Was I able to gain a full appreciation of what is "right and good" for this situation? . . . I was relying on my colleague's notes . . . they seemed ok . . . but sometimes the notes are out of date and misleading . . . How can I try and address this? . . . Perhaps I can make a point of checking the dates for the last contact . . . or maybe I can do some research about this client's condition . . .'.

ACTIVITY **1.1**

Professional reasoning

Use one of the principles above to explore a small area of your practice where you made a judgement call. Note what is happening as you do this.

Does it help you focus on your reasoning and judgement processes?

By using the practical reasoning principles in this way, professional judgement can be explored in more depth and areas of development more readily identified for CPD purposes. As has been seen earlier, professional capability and the quality of practice have individual and elusive natures which makes specifying and defining them for learning or assessment purposes tricky (Collins and Daly, 2011: 4). However, by understanding and articulating the practical reasoning behind professional judgement, this problem can be alleviated to a degree. We will come back to this in Chapter 4 when we look at reflection for CPD.

Of course, these practical reasoning principles are still vague in themselves; for example, you might ask what 'sound' moral judgement is exactly. The point is that the detail should be explored and considered within the context of a specific situation. If the principles were predetermined, they would not be able to be defined for particular circumstances and requirements, and it would deny your obligation, as a professional, to do so.

Knowledge and judgement

Another key but sometimes indefinable aspect of professional judgement is the use of knowledge. For O'Sullivan (2006), practice wisdom is the ability to integrate different types of knowledge in ways that facilitate sound judgement. This should allow for an equal relationship between theory and practice, which was seen earlier as necessary for professional capability. However, in a technocratic model, theory or research is seen to direct practice in a rather one-way approach, and this can ignore the input or agency of the practitioner in critically using that knowledge. There is now, more than ever, a need to move away from approaches which have this emphasis on technical rationality and a simple deductive 'application' of theory or evidence to practice (Eraut, 1985). This is because they reduce a practitioner to the level of a technician following set instructions and procedures in an uncritical fashion. Such technical 'fixes' can also reduce the complex issues of social work practice to a type of problem that can be solved with set instructions and routine procedures. In effect, they align with a competency-based approach rather than a capability one.

As Thompson and Pascal (2012: 314) state, the professional knowledge base 'offers helpful insights but not simple or direct lines of action for practice' or indeed a foolproof way of identifying the issues correctly in the first place. Any knowledge or evidence, whether academic, from colleagues, or based on your own experience, can only help you explore and explain a situation and its potential resolutions, and inform your practical reasoning and judgement. It should not dictate the way forward. If we return to our earlier example, a particular model may suggest a partnership approach for agreeing objectives within per-formance management, but this could easily be interpreted as tokenistic or even insulting by someone who thinks they may soon be made redundant. Knowledge has to be critically evaluated in respect of the context and situation it is being used for. Intuition and other elusive elements will also be at play to make sense of any patterns and fill the gaps in knowledge and understanding. Again, this is a rather intangible activity. Thompson and Pascal (2012: 311) note that we 'have only a beginning of understanding of what actually happens when knowledge is integrated into practice in a meaningful way or how knowledge is generated from practice'.

For Collins and Daly (2011), the relationship between knowledge or evidence and professional judgement is crucial, and should be as transparent as possible because we have to understand what makes decision-making a sound process and what mechanisms are required to support it. Oko (2011: xiii) sees the need to consider 'knowledge as process' rather than 'knowledge as product' and to see knowledge as something that develops by an 'active involvement in using it'. This activity benefits greatly from being sensitively – but also critically – guided and explored, in dialogue with others.

Such active and critical use of knowledge will start to produce your own 'knowledge': the understanding gained from such processes, especially if you are articulating learning outputs for CPD purposes. Existing knowledge will be reviewed and new knowledge received but it will also be generated for a particular situation. For Tynjälä et al. (2003), for example, it is specifically this process which produces 'practice-based theory'. To use our example for a final time, you may well have researched, reasoned through and created a uniquely sensitive approach to the performance management of the person under the threat of restructuring and redundancy. It would be wrong, therefore, to think that such production of knowledge is an uncritical process or that it is constructing mere opinion. Taylor and White (2001) argue that it is rigorous because you will be analysing the authority of any knowledge and the claims being used and produced. It becomes valid and robust if you engage in a process of critical thinking and reflection; allowing a full exploration and justification of your practical reasoning, thoughts and emotions (Noble, 2001). To put it another way, you need to take a 'helicopter' view of your practice and look at it critically from a distance as well as from within. It gives an opportunity to explore this knowledge use and construction process, and to learn to trust it.

In conclusion, professionalism concerns judgement, reasoning and the critical use of a range of knowledge. In turn, this 'process of systematically reflecting on one's own professional practice and discerning alternative and improved ways of resolving professional concerns' will produce a practical but still valid type of knowledge (Guile and Young, 1996: 172). These ideas will be explored further as we discuss learning in more detail in Chapter 3.

What do we mean by the term 'professional development'?

As professional activity is so complex, the more discussion there is around practice and capability, the better. Talking about practice, especially within a culture of learning, helps us to become more aware of particular aspects or nuances of professional thinking, decision-making and action. The development of professional expertise is said to come from building up a 'bank' of experience and range of examples, which are then used to help form strategies for dealing with new experiences. It is not about repeatedly following prescribed routines or having a stock of procedures which are then retrieved and rigidly followed. Your expertise and confidence comes from continually creating 'new' practice to fit situations and continually learning from this, with the latter benefitting from shared reflection, exploration and feedback (Boshuizen *et al.*, 2004).

By incorporating the principles of professional capability and the notion of quality of work, the development of professional practice becomes more than a review of actions or processes. Ongoing examination and improvement of both thinking and practical abilities leads to new understanding and perspectives of your practice and service quality. Professional development therefore concerns a process of conscious experiential learning *from* doing rather than *by* doing alone (Jones and Joss, 1995: 25), which, in turn, requires a deeper level of commitment and self-awareness from you.

What do we mean by the term 'continuing professional development'?

The Social Work Task Force (2009: 15) suggests that the social work profession should be made up of highly skilled qualified practitioners whose expertise continually develops throughout their careers.

Skills for Care defines CPD as:

> *planned learning and development activity that develops, maintains or extends knowledge, skills, understanding or performance. It can include a wide range of activity, designed to equip a worker to provide quality social care and/or support their career development.*
>
> (SWRB, 2010: 1)

O'Sullivan (2006: 1) takes a wider view of CPD as the 'learning in which professionals engage in the context of their working lives', meeting the needs of the professional, the employer, the profession and society itself. So the idea is that development of professionalism is ongoing, and it may be planned or undertaken on a more ad hoc basis. CPD therefore involves a range of learning (formal and informal) that maintains and enhances professional practice and service quality, but can also extend and advance practice for career progression purposes. By taking into account the notion of capability explained earlier, we can see that continuing learning and development at a professional level involves more than updating knowledge and skills through basic training (although this is, of course, extremely important); it is also about reconsidering the ability to make sound judgements and decisions. It involves engagement with, and critical reflection on, experience, which facilitates the promotion of professional values and principles which guide action (Tyreman, 2000: 122).

Attitudes to CPD

To undertake CPD as an ongoing, continuing and inherent part of practice can appear quite onerous, and so there has to be an intrinsic reward for anyone undertaking it. Cooper (2008: 222) argues that 'the attitudes of professional workers to their CPD is a strong indicator, if not a defining feature, of their approach to practice'. There is a fundamental link in how CPD is viewed and its impact on you – it is about the quality of your working life. If CPD is viewed as something done to you, or you take the view to only do the minimum required, it will probably be seen as an additional burden on top of the 'real' work you are doing. Any involvement will become superficial or at worse, resented. If, instead, it is seen as part of your professional role and 'owned', it is likely to be much more meaningful and relevant to your work and have a positive impact on your practice, and on you in a more general sense. I am sure that most practitioners do want to engage with it in the best way, but it is perhaps not always the easiest option to take in the real world. Nevertheless, you do have some choice in the attitude you take to CPD. Cooper (2011) provides different illustrations of the connection between social work careers and attitudes to CPD, using seven different metaphors; for example, CPD seen as a journey or through relationships with others. The need is to adopt an appropriate level of responsibility and understand the complexities, contributions and capabilities of your best practice in connection with CPD; that is, your personal relationship to it.

What is clear from the research, though, is that proactive learning is underpinned by a number of very important things. Overall there is a need to take good care of yourself, to have thought through a strategy for maintaining your wellbeing from the beginning (Seden and McCormick, 2011). Such learning also benefits greatly from the expertise and insight of supportive employers and training/education providers and colleagues (Davis *et al.*, 2011), points to which we will return in later chapters.

FURTHER READING

Adams, R., Dominelli, L. and Payne, R. (2009) *Critical Practice in Social Work*, 2nd edn. Basingstoke: Palgrave Macmillan.

Bondi, L., Carr, D., Clark, C. and Clegg C. (eds) (2011) *Towards Professional Wisdom: Practical Deliberation in the People Professions*. Farnham: Ashgate.

Taylor, B. (2010) *Professional Decision Making in Social Work*. Exeter: Learning Matters.

Chapter 2
A CPD learning cycle

In this chapter, a process for undertaking CPD is encouraged so that it can be set within an appropriate learning framework. The PCF is explored in more detail to see how the domains and levels associated with professional social work practice might be used to set learning and development objectives. This can help you undertake CPD in a way that ensures all your learning counts.

In many ways it does not matter if CPD is undertaken formally or informally, as long as it is undertaken within an overall process that allows both to result in meaningful learning and rewarding outputs.

CPD processes usually involve four key stages in an ongoing cycle, as shown in Figure 2.1.

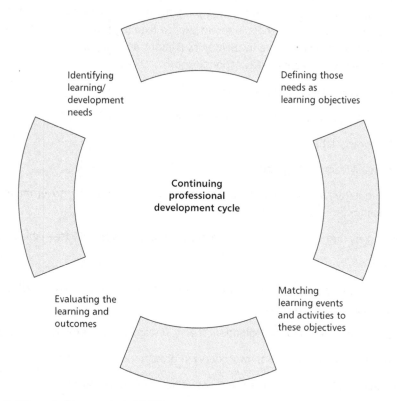

Identifying learning/ development needs

Defining those needs as learning objectives

Continuing professional development cycle

Evaluating the learning and outcomes

Matching learning events and activities to these objectives

Figure 2.1 CPD cycle (Brown et al., 2012)

The key points, based on O'Sullivan (2006) are:

- the process needs to be planned to some extent;
- there is a need for analysis, action and review throughout;
- the individual is primarily responsible for managing and undertaking his/her CPD activity;
- learning objectives serve organisational as well as individual goals or needs.

Learning objectives are the pivotal elements within this cycle. They usually state what you hope to be able to do as a result of your learning and they will start with the particular needs and requirements for your practice role, as well as those of your team and the wider organisation. Analysing and then defining these learning and development needs as personal goals translates them into distinct learning objectives. Learning objectives are easier to match to particular learning opportunities (whether they are in-house, through higher education, research or project work), and also easier to reflect on, evaluate and review.

Setting learning objectives for developing the scope of any work being undertaken – the roles, tasks, processes and procedures – will be relatively easier than setting them for developing the quality of work. As we have seen, the latter is not so easy to define. This is where you may need to be less prescriptive but identify relevant 'markers' which show change and development. The elements of professional judgement and principles of practical reasoning seen in the last chapter may help here. It is important to allow space and opportunities for unexpected and unplanned learning too, not ignore it just because it was not specified at the start. The danger of pre-planning and pre-organising too much is that it can sometimes destroy the potential for learning. Some people resent explicit learning but will naturally like to find new solutions and be very creative in their work (Simons and Ruijters, 2001). It is therefore better to let at least some learning occur spontaneously.

As far as possible, learning objectives should:

(a) State content/topic areas. This can relate to relevant:

- areas of new legislation or policy;
- organisational/team strategy and goals;
- sets of regulatory or advisory standards of practice produced by government, quasi-government or professional organisations.

For social workers they should also relate to particular domains in the PCF (see Table 2.1).

(b) Be holistic.

To incorporate the notion of professional capability, objectives need to allow for all interconnected aspects of practice:

- knowledge and understanding (legislation, theory, research, policy, experiential wisdom);
- skills and doing (thinking, actions, procedures, processes, practice abilities);
- values and being (aware of own assumptions, ethics, morals, and so on).

Table 2.1 PCF domains

PCF domains

At the time of writing (July 2012) the PCF domains are detailed as follows by The College:

1. Professionalism – Identify and behave as a professional social worker, committed to professional development.

Social workers are members of an internationally recognised profession, a title protected in UK law. Social workers demonstrate professional commitment by taking responsibility for their conduct, practice and learning, with support through supervision. As representatives of the social work profession, they safeguard its reputation and are accountable to the professional regulator.

2. Values and ethics – Apply social work ethical principles and values to guide professional practice.

Social workers have an obligation to conduct themselves ethically and to engage in ethical decision-making, including through partnership with people who use their services. Social workers are knowledgeable about the value base of their profession, its ethical standards and relevant law.

3. Diversity – Recognise diversity and apply anti-discriminatory and anti-oppressive principles in practice.

Social workers understand that diversity is a natural and normal feature of all human kind. Diversity is multi-dimensional and includes race, disability, class, economic status, age, sexual orientation, sex and gender, transgender, and religion or belief. Social workers appreciate that, as a consequence of difference, a person's life experience may include oppression, marginalisation and alienation as well as privilege, power and acclaim, and are able to challenge, support and advocate appropriately.

4. Rights, Justice and Economic Wellbeing – Advance human rights and promote social justice and economic wellbeing.

Social workers recognise the fundamental principles of human rights and equality, and that these are protected in national and international law, conventions and policies. They ensure these principles underpin their practice. Social workers understand the importance of using and contributing to case law and applying these rights in their own practice. They understand the effects of oppression, discrimination and poverty.

5. Knowledge – Apply knowledge of social sciences, law and social work practice theory.

Social workers understand psychological, social, cultural, spiritual and physical influences on people; human development throughout the life span and the legal framework for practice. They apply this knowledge in their work with individuals, families and communities. They know and use theories and methods of social work practice.

6. Critical Reflection and Analysis – Apply critical reflection and analysis to inform and provide a rationale for professional decision-making.

Table 2.1 Continued

PCF domains

Social workers are knowledgeable about and apply the principles of critical thinking and reasoned discernment. They identify, distinguish, evaluate and integrate multiple sources of knowledge and evidence. These include practice evidence, their own practice experience, service user and carer experience, together with research-based, organisational, policy and legal knowledge. They use critical thinking augmented by creativity and curiosity.

7. Intervention and Skills – Use judgement and authority to intervene with individuals, families and communities to promote independence, provide support and prevent harm, neglect and abuse.

Social workers engage with individuals, families, groups and communities, working alongside people to assess and intervene. They enable effective relationships and are effective communicators, using appropriate skills. Using their professional judgement, they employ a range of interventions: promoting independence, providing support and protection, taking preventative action and ensuring safety whilst balancing rights and risks. They understand and take account of differentials in power, and are able to use authority appropriately. They evaluate their own practice and the outcomes for those they work with.

8. Contexts and Organisations – Engage with, inform, and adapt to changing contexts that shape practice. Operate effectively within own organisational frameworks and contribute to the development of services and organisations. Operate effectively within multi-agency and inter-professional settings.

Social workers are informed about and proactively responsive to the challenges and opportunities that come with changing social contexts and constructs. They fulfil this responsibility in accordance with their professional values and ethics, both as individual professionals and as members of the organisations in which they work. They collaborate, inform and are informed by their work with others, inter-professionally and with communities.

9. Professional Leadership – Take responsibility for the professional learning and development of others through supervision, mentoring, assessing, research, teaching, leadership and management.

The social work profession evolves through the contribution of its members in activities such as practice research, supervision, assessment of practice, teaching and management. An individual's contribution will gain influence when undertaken as part of a learning, practice-focused organisation. Learning may be facilitated with a wide range of people including social work colleagues, service users and carers, volunteers, foster carers and other professionals.

Available from: **www.collegeofsocialwork.org/pcf.aspx**
It is essential to visit The College website for up-to-date and more detailed material.

(c) Define the level of thinking/learning/output.

Levels of thinking, learning and output can be difficult to clarify at the outset, but essentially it is about being aware of the differences between surface and deep learning, which are detailed in the following chapter; an example is the difference between knowing about particularly relevant sections of the Mental Capacity Act and being able to use and interpret them when assessing a vulnerable person.

For social workers, the PCF is divided into levels, both before and after qualification. The levels relate to the complexity of work that someone with those capabilities would be able to manage. Progression between levels within the PCF is determined by the ability to manage issues such as complexity, risk and responsibility in a range of professional settings, and so these may be useful indicators to identify at the outset here.

Table 2.2 Progression between PCF levels

Progression between PCF levels

At the time of writing (July 2012), The College notes these particular issues to think about. After each issue is outlined, there are some questions that can help you identify where there may be gaps in your expertise or where further progression needs to take place.

Level of confidence, underpinned by practice experience, reflection and deepening understanding.

- What do I feel confident about and why? What did experience, theory, reflection or other people contribute? How?

The increasing ability to work independently and to collaborate on equal terms with members of other professions.

- Who do I work with? Do they operate within a different set of values or principles? How do I work with the medical/social model and how does this affect my attitude to the people who work with it?

The quality of the judgements made, and the level of ability to explain and justify them.

- How can I use the practical reasoning principles to evaluate the quality of my judgements? What else can I use that is appropriate?

Efficacy of the work undertaken and the outcomes achieved, including opportunities for preventive work.

- Who can I get meaningful feedback from to review this?

The ability to take initiative, form constructive alliances and to act as a change agent.

- Where have I made a difference and how?

The ability to engage effectively with situations of increasing complexity and challenge, for example those with:

- multi-agency input
- complex family/organisational dynamics

Table 2.2 Continued

Progression between PCF levels

- serious hostility and conflicts of interest
- multiple problems/disadvantages
- multiple/significant risk factors
- need to take into account the public interest
- What was the complexity I engaged with and how did I react?

The appropriate use of authority and challenge.

- What type of situation requires me to assert my authority; or make challenges? Why? How can/do I do this in the best way? What do I need to avoid doing?

The ability and commitment to educate and provide professional supervision to others.

- Which principles of supervision am I adhering to? How? What do supervisees truly think of my style?

Demonstration of leadership, management and research.

- How can I develop some meaningful 'markers' to show what I have achieved – what do others, such as professional societies, say is good leadership, management or research?

Available from: **www.collegeofsocialwork.org/pcf.aspx**
It is essential to visit the website for up-to-date and more detailed material.

Having some concrete professional or workplace targets helps make the learning processes more meaningful and productive for CPD purposes; it gives a clear focus and also helps intensify and sustain learning. In addition, because these learning objectives are then reviewed and evaluated, it becomes easier to note particular development and change (i.e. the learning that has occurred) and its impact on your practice, performance and on service quality. The cycle supports the output model of CPD very well.

ACTIVITY **2.1**

Plans and learning objectives

Produce a work-based personal development/improvement plan for yourself with your line manager/supervisor/appraiser or other appropriate person. Identify your key learning objectives for CPD purposes.

FURTHER READING

Skills for Care website (**www.skillsforcare.org.uk**). For further help and advice, use the 'developing skills' section where practical guides, support templates and advice are available for effective continuing professional development for adult social care workers.

Seden, J., Matthews, S., McCormick, M. and Morgan, A. (eds) (2011) *Professional Development in Social Work.* London: Routledge.

Chapter 3
Learning for CPD

Now that we have looked at an appropriate process, it is necessary to consider the type of learning that best suits the particular nature of CPD we are discussing here. This chapter reviews self-managed learning, learning styles and experiential learning, but first it explores the level of learning and the best approaches to knowledge and learning that can help to bring about change and development in your practice.

What type of learning is involved?

To start, we can use work by Simons and Ruijters (2001), who note that professionals are undertaking different types of learning and highlight some useful distinctions here.

* Learning implicitly in and from practice, and building on skills and capabilities so that everyday experiences shape professional judgement and practice. They call this *elaboration*.

* Learning explicitly (e.g. from training or theory/research) and increasing skills, ideas and conceptual understanding. They call this *expansion*.

* Contributing to the development of the profession and to team/organisational learning by becoming aware of the outcomes of their implicit/explicit learning and articulating their insights. They call this *externalising*.

It is useful to be aware of and recognise distinctions such as these, especially implicit and explicit learning, but you also need to be aware of the different levels of learning. As seen earlier, CPD should lead to a new understanding and perspective of practice, and we can explore how this can be achieved in more detail now.

ACTIVITY **3.1**

Levels of learning

Which of these descriptions matches your view of what learning is?

A. *Learning as an increase in knowledge or skills.*

B. *Learning as memorising or storing knowledge or skills which can be reproduced or recalled in their original state.*

C. *Learning as* acquiring *knowledge or skills that can be retained and used as necessary, but which are limited in* providing 'set answers' *to routine problems in practice.*

D. *Learning as* making sense or understanding meaning *for ourselves. Involves breaking knowledge down and identifying what is significant and why. It is about combining ideas and thinking creatively, to understand and resolve complex problems in practice.*

E. *Learning as interpreting and understanding the world in a different way, by re-interpreting knowledge and therefore* creating *it too. It is about being able to take account of the underlying uncertainty, contingency and restraints of practice.*

Adapted from Säljö (1979)

Of course, learning can be all or any of these descriptions. In fact, level E best fits the type of learning expected for meaningful CPD but this means that a particular matching view of whatever it is you are learning (we can refer to this as knowledge in its widest sense) is also necessary. In effect, you will need to view knowledge as something that you can validly 'construct' through this experience. This idea was introduced in the previous chapter and we can explore it in more detail here.

Ways to view knowledge

A simplistic view of knowledge and learning

A 'traditional' but inappropriate way of viewing knowledge is to see it as something certain and absolute, usually in the hands of experts; that is, as right or already established answers. This absolutist view leads to a situation where answers are not worked through for yourself, and those answers obtained from other people are not questioned. So, for example, it would result in a theory or piece of research being described within written work and used to merely support ideas (i.e. working at levels A–C above), rather than being interpreted or critically explored (i.e. levels D–E). It would also mean that an over-reliance would be placed on colleagues' notes or advice.

Another inappropriate view of knowledge is to see that there are many right answers out there (a multiplist view) and to see all the answers as equally valid and never commit to any of them. These views do not encourage practitioners to think for themselves either, or learn to apply reasoned judgement to knowledge and develop individual expertise. They will not help deal with the complexity of practice in a capable and professional way or learn from an engagement with it. Of course, issues regarding confidence and experience play an important part here – novice practitioners will naturally rely on others more, but we do need to question how far that reliance should extend.

New knowledge and information may be presented in such ways to you though, as something given and received but not to be critically engaged with. This is a problem because we tend to engage with knowledge in the way it is presented to us or in the way we are assessed on our understanding of it. This is associated with the idea of a *surface approach* to learning (Marton and Säljö, 1976; Prosser and Trigwell, 1999). This is why I would argue it is not productive to undertake practice learning using a simplistic competency-based approach, even for new knowledge and understanding, because it will not align with the approach necessary for continuing learning. A person needs to be enabled to understand and feel confident with any new knowledge or skill in a way which does not develop over-reliance on it as a 'truth', otherwise it will never be able to be critically evaluated or made sense of individually.

Much training (as opposed to education) is by nature only aiming for initial understanding rather than deeper thinking and engagement, although there are exceptions. Training can provide basic ideas or methods but may not be concerned with wider and more critical debates around the topic itself, or with deeper and more theoretical ideas and research. Training at its most basic level will be unlikely to provide you with alternative ideas to critically consider, or encourage you to evaluate these ideas in practice or to critically discuss this with others. Therefore, to enhance such learning with deeper thinking and more meaningful engagement requires you to adopt a more advanced view of knowledge and learning, defined below.

Of course, if CPD is being undertaken in a higher education learning environment or within a formal practice learning situation, it would be hoped that a deeper and more meaningful engagement is apparent in the teaching, learning support and assessment activities. Even so, a more conscious understanding of learning and an ability to adopt the right approach yourself is still necessary, and we can see how this can be achieved below.

Adopting a more advanced view of knowledge and learning

So far we have seen that undertaking CPD should encourage you to interpret, adapt and evaluate knowledge in use, and produce ideas of your own as a result. You have the right, and also the responsibility, as a professional to reason through and evaluate knowledge or methods in respect of how well they 'perform' in particular practice situations, and then articulate the outcome as your new understanding and as valid knowledge.

Therefore, in contrast to the surface approach mentioned above, undertaking CPD should allow you to develop a *deep approach* (Marton and Säljö, 1976) to the subject matter (and to the learning) and enable you to take a more critical and evaluative stance to knowledge and learning. It is about using other people's ideas (e.g. theory or a senior colleague's expertise) for illumination rather than support. You will be researching, using and appraising a wide range of knowledge during CPD activities, and by doing this you will start to develop your own ideas, understanding, insight and unique interpretations: that is, new knowledge.

To reiterate, the key is to think about knowledge as being able to be interpreted for different situations and to be constructed for them too. New knowledge (or knowing) gets its validity by being the 'best option' for the situation in hand. This new knowledge can, however, still be challenged in the future, as you remain open to other ideas and the changing context. This is called *contextual knowing* (Baxter Magolda, 1996). The main point is that any type of knowledge should not be seen as something certain and absolute, or solely in the hands of experts or academics; it should also be able to be challenged or evaluated in respect of the situation it is being used for. We can see how well this aligns with our notion of capability and how these processes form part of practical reasoning and judgement, as explored in Chapter 1.

The point is reiterated by Mathews and Crawford when they say that:

> *the process of 'doing' and 'understanding' creates and adds to our knowledge . . . we must be open to emerging knowledge and be willing to adopt a questioning stance that recognises that our existing evidence base is never complete and that the search for knowledge is an ongoing quest.*

> (2011: 14–15)

These authors also argue that practice wisdom and other sources of informal knowledge have an important contribution to make to effective practice because they can recognise the uncertainty and ambiguity inherent in practice. Of course, use of such informal sources involves continually questioning and reflecting on interpretations, filtering differing kinds of subjective evidence and information – such as intuition, feelings, past experience, personal/professional values – with a more objective use of reason and critical thinking.

Adams *et al.* agree, and argue that professional expertise is about building knowledge in and for different situations:

> *professional expertise involves the ability to create knowledge from experience in context and the ability to transfer this knowledge to different situations. Expertise . . . is learnt in context but what is developed is knowledge which allows this learning to be applied successfully in new and diverse situations.*

> (2009: 240)

In other words, the understanding and wisdom which we develop in specific practice situations can be used in a range of other situations because we are constantly developing and adapting it. They call it *contextual knowledge development*.

This way of looking at knowledge contextually (critically constructing valid meaning for yourself and being able to develop a confident 'knowing' for different situations) aligns well with the critical, questioning and open stance needed for the development of professional capability. This deep approach is better able to take account of uncertain and complex situations; it requires self-motivated and reflective learners, engaged holistically in self-directed, ongoing learning.

ACTIVITY **3.2**

Exploring a deep approach to learning

Think about the ideas being presented here.

- *Do they match your own ideas about learning and knowledge?*

- *Write a statement which starts to describe a deep learning approach for yourself. Make a note of any queries or issues – try to work through these with a supervisor or with colleagues.*

Self-managed learning

The notion of taking responsibility for your CPD is extremely pivotal, especially for managers and leaders; as Hock (2000) says, the primary responsibility of anyone who has a managerial role is to manage self. It is about taking responsibility for your learning and development rather than relying on your organisation to drive this and your career. It involves you in your own 'curriculum planning' if you like, designing the structure and content of what is learnt and the process of learning itself.

This type of learning relies and builds on some of our earlier ideas about learning and knowledge. As we saw, viewing knowledge contextually aligns well with the critical, questioning and open stance needed for professional capability and CPD. Within self-managed learning, it means that you will not only be taking responsibility for gathering and using knowledge, information and ideas from a range of different sources, you will also be responsible for taking a 'deep learning' approach (Marton and Säljö, 1976) to it all. For example, it is up to you to decide what to read, which theories are important and why, where research may be located and how relevant it is, or how policies or legislation can be interpreted. It will also be up to you to put this learning into operation in the workplace in order to demonstrate practice development abilities.

Self-managed learning is about seeing learning as something you actively take part in and help design; it cannot be viewed in a traditional manner of expecting a 'teacher' or 'manager' to provide you with a complete package of aims and content (i.e. the specific outcomes, all the materials, ideas and routes) and you as the 'pupil' to receive them and then replicate them somehow. It puts you firmly in the driving seat of the journey. In effect if you are expecting someone else to decide on your destination and the route taken and provide the petrol, you will not be going anywhere! On the other hand, you are not alone on this journey; other people (e.g. a colleague, supervisor, mentor) can act as the co-driver providing a range of materials and ideas, plus essential guidance, advice, support and encouragement. We will explore this further in Chapter 5 when we look at learning environments for CPD.

Taking a critical approach to self-managed learning

The skills of self-managed learning will involve you in:

1. taking the initiative in diagnosing your learning needs;

2. recognising and capturing the learning potential of everyday events;

3. critically reflecting on practice and its outcomes;

4. creating your own learning objectives;

5. identifying, locating and evaluating the resources needed;

6. choosing and implementing appropriate learning strategies;

7. evaluating learning outcomes;

8. digesting and generalising learning in order to facilitate its transfer.

These are useful skills but, as with any process, a more holistic and critical stance can foster an even deeper approach and therefore a more meaningful engagement. In everyday language, being critical can mean finding fault and being negative about something. In this situation it is a more positive and constructive idea – it is about not taking things for granted, and not accepting how a situation seems or is portrayed. It is about questioning and evaluating any claims, and it can lead to far-reaching outcomes (Mingers, 2000). The skills and abilities of self-directed learners listed above, therefore, can be enhanced by adding certain questions that a critical approach brings.

1. Take the initiative in diagnosing your learning needs.

   By taking a critical approach you can also ask:

   - What type of information informs this diagnosis – feedback, evaluation, meetings, reactions, gut feeling . . .?
   - Who provides the input and how – colleagues, supervisors, managers, other learners . . .?
   - How honest and informed am I about my areas of strength and weakness?
   - What prompts me to take action, and what stops me?

2. Recognise and capture the learning potential of everyday events.

   By taking a critical approach you can also ask:

   - How and when do I note colleagues' ideas, tips, methods of working as useful or as areas of need within my own working practices?
   - If a staff member is not performing well, how do I analyse my part of the responsibility?

3. Critically reflect on your practice and its outcomes.

   By taking a critical approach you can also ask:

   - Who critically questions me?
   - How open am I to new perspectives?
   - Have I actively sought a direct observation of my practice?
   - Do I record my reflection and use it for my learning?
   - Do I ensure my reflection is strengths-based as well?

4. Create your own learning objectives.

   By taking a critical approach you can also ask:

   - How do I use any input or feedback to form objectives?
   - Do I discuss them with anyone?

5. Identify, locate and evaluate the resources needed.

   By taking a critical approach you can also ask:

   - What happens if the resources are not there?
   - How can I make sure my time is protected for researching new ideas, etc.?

- Who else could help me?

- What other options are there?

6. Choose and implement appropriate learning strategies.

   By taking a critical approach you can also ask:

   - Do I review a full range of styles and approaches as well as my particular preferences?

   - How do I ensure that new knowledge, skills or ideas from training are put into practice and not left as a bunch of notes or handouts?

   - How do I try to overcome the negativity associated with an organisation or team culture that is not conducive to learning?

7. Evaluate learning outcomes.

   By taking a critical approach you can also ask:

   - Do I revisit my learning objectives?

   - Do I test out whether my practice has changed and how?

   - Do I actively seek and reflect on more critical feedback from service users or colleagues in order to gain a different perspective?

   - Do I reflect on feedback from assessed work undertaken within formal programmes of study?

   - No one can be expected to practise perfectly – how do I judge whether my aims and expectations are set too high?

8. Digest and generalise learning in order to facilitate its transfer.

   By taking a critical approach you can also ask:

   - When I reflect on the learning gained from a specific situation, do I start to articulate it in more general ideas and concepts? For example: 'I want to use the reflective question my supervisor used on me with other colleagues – it was a really effective deep learning prompt . . .'

   - Do I make connections between different areas of learning and different situations looking for common elements?

   Based on Williams and Rutter (2010: 129–30)

As can be seen, it is necessary to understand your methods of learning and preferred styles here. A range of different learning styles will probably need to be adopted for CPD because there are so many aspects to it. It is important to understand whether you have any strong preferences and whether a particular area needs supporting or enhancing.

Understanding your learning style

There are many different models, but the best known is perhaps Honey and Mumford's (1982), which identifies four main learning styles.

- Activist
  - enthusiastic for new experiences and may rush into them;
  - can get hooked on what is happening in front of them;
  - may get bored by having to stop and consolidate ideas;
  - can centre everything on themselves – even group discussion.

Activists will prefer new experiences, short activities with plenty of variety, situations where they are in the spotlight, being allowed to talk about new ideas, and to have a go at things.

- Reflector
  - observes and evaluates experiences from several different perspectives;
  - collects data and considers evidence before deciding on action;
  - may be overly cautious and distant;
  - likes to fully understand a discussion before making their point;
  - may seem distant but tolerant.

Reflectors will prefer situations where they can watch and think about activities, carry out investigations or research before acting, review the evidence, and produce their own considered report or action plan. They will need plenty of time for decisions.

- Pragmatist
  - enjoys experimentation and practical application of ideas and theories;
  - can get frustrated by open-ended discussion;
  - prefers active problem solving;
  - sees opportunities as a challenge;
  - may also rush into action;
  - tends to look for better or more practical ways of doing things.

Pragmatists will prefer practical courses where there is an obvious link between their job and the learning offered. They will like to try things out with coaching and feedback. They will need to integrate any theory they have learnt into practice quickly so you can see its relevance.

- Theorist
  - will usually think through problems logically and systematically;
  - can be perfectionist;
  - likes to analyse;
  - may not be able to think laterally;
  - can prefer certainty to subjective judgement;
  - may be detached and analytical.

Theorists will prefer activities where there are plans, maps or models to describe what is happening. They need time to explore things carefully so that they understand how things are done in detail and look for structured information.

This is one of the best recognised models but there are other types of learning styles that have been identified, such as the VAK (or VARK) learning style indicators which highlight preferred skills and abilities for learning associated with visual aspects (preferring to see a demonstration or a diagram), auditory aspects (preferring verbal instructions or talking something through) and kinaesthetic aspects (preferring to try things out yourself first).

There is considerable debate surrounding learning styles and their use that suggests a high level of unreliability (Smith, 2001; Coffield *et al.*, 2004), so they need to be used critically and in an open, non-prescriptive way.

ACTIVITY 3.3

Learning styles

Consider the type of learner you are and if you have a preferred style of learning.

You will find information about learning styles using a basic web search or use **www.businessballs.com** for the VAK materials. Use the material found critically – do not try to pigeon-hole or label yourself.

In effect, most people find they are a mixture of different styles, but, as stated above, it is worth considering if you have a dominant preference because CPD relies on being able to adopt all these learning styles. You may need to seek additional support to help with your least preferred styles. For example, if you prefer to learn by doing (i.e. just getting stuck in and then moving on to the next task), you may need to seek support to develop a more reflective approach in order to consolidate, develop and articulate your understanding from these experiences. If you prefer to reflect, read and discuss things but are anxious about more practical involvement, you may need to seek support in order to gain the confidence or courage necessary to get on and do things.

In addition, it can be argued that there is a need for a balance across all styles in order to work at a professional level. Any dominant preference for just one style could impact negatively on performance and practice development. For example, a project manager needs to not only be able to theorise and problem solve but also reflect, take some risk in trying something out and also get personally involved.

Maximising the learning from experience

As we saw at the start of this chapter and in the Introduction, implicit learning from experience is important in CPD. Implicit or informal learning covers events like observation, feedback, dialogue and co-working, and usually results in new knowing or understanding that is either tacit or regarded as part of a person's general capability, rather than as something learnt. It is a key area for professional development; for example, Eraut (1994) suggests that something like 80 per cent of all learning happens in this way.

However, it is not enough to have experiences and passively expect to learn from them. It is important to take an active approach to implicit learning within practice, and engage in all aspects of planning, undertaking, monitoring, reflecting on and evaluating your learning (Jarvis, 1992). This is about bringing an attitude of enquiry to experience and asking yourself how you actually developed your interpretation of any events. Recognising the need to make the most of informal as well as more formal learning to develop practice becomes a critical habit of mind (Rutter and Brown, 2011).

Making implicit learning more explicit and meaningful is helped by approaching it a bit more systematically and using a CPD cycle (see Chapter 2) to plan for it, record it, reflect on it, actively use the ideas in practice and evaluate the outcomes. Using experiential learning models can also help maximise work-based learning – here are two models for consideration.

1. Race (2010) – 'ripples' model

In this holistic model, each element interacts with the others like ripples in a pond, creating an integrated interacting 'whole' which constitutes successful learning:

- *wanting* = motivation for learning;

- *doing* = practice, trial and error;

- *digesting* = making sense of it, reflecting on it, gaining ownership;

- *feedback* = seeing the results, other people's reactions.

The internal circle of 'wanting' sends ripples of motivation out through all the surrounding layers. If we are not motivated then we are usually not learning well or very deeply. Similarly, the external circle of 'feedback' sends ripples back into the model from the various sources

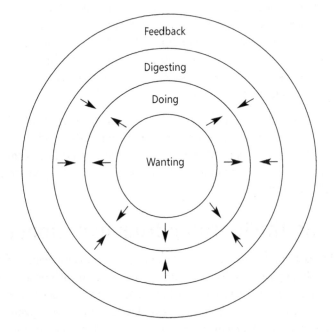

Figure 3.1 Race's 'ripples' model

which provide it (e.g. instructors, fellow learners, assessment, etc.). 'Doing' and 'digesting', on the other hand, are regarded as overlapping processes that are continuously influenced both by motivation and by feedback. The idea is to ensure the inner and outer circles are in place for learning to be maximised.

2. Kolb (1984) – experiential learning model

In this alternative model, there is a cycle of learning with four elements:

- a concrete experience;
- reflective observation (reviewing and reflecting on the experience);
- abstract conceptualisation (concluding and learning from the experience);
- active experimentation (planning and trying out what has been learnt).

The cycle may be entered at any stage and it perpetuates itself. For effective learning to take place, all four stages of the cycle should be planned for and made use of. Concrete experience should be followed by reflection on that experience, which is then followed by the consideration of general ideas and concepts describing the experience, or the linking of known theories to it (abstract conceptualisation), and hence to the planning of the next occurrence of the experience (active experimentation), leading in turn to the next concrete experience. As a learner you move from being an active participant, to an observer, to an analyst and then to an experimenter.

ACTIVITY **3.4**

Experiential learning

Think about which model you like best and why. Can you relate any particular parts to your own work-based learning experiences?

Which elements from each model do you think are essential to maximise learning from experience? Why? What essential part do they play and how can you ensure you include them for when you learn in this way or for when you enable others?

By understanding more about learning as a subject in itself, you can start to understand your own learning better and begin to develop a conscious awareness of it. In my own experience, whenever I teach a unit on enabling the learning of others, many participants state that they wish they'd understood some of these principles earlier in the course, or even in their lives. For them, and for myself too, exploring the emotion and the techniques of learning helps to clarify and improve the whole experience.

FURTHER READING

Beverley, A. and Worsley, A. (2007) *Learning and Teaching in Social Work Practice*. London: Palgrave Macmillan.

Lishman, J. (2011) *Social Work Education and Training*. London: Jessica Kingsley.

Walker, J., Crawford, K. and Parker, J. (2008) *Practice Education in Social Work: A Handbook for Practice Teachers, Assessors and Educators*. Exeter: Learning Matters.

Williams, S. and Rutter, L. (2010) *The Practice Educator's Handbook*. Exeter: Learning Matters.

Chapter 4
Reflection for CPD

As we have seen, CPD is enhanced by adopting the best approach to this type of learning and by using appropriate methods. This level of engagement with CPD is improved further with the use of critical reflection. This chapter reviews ideas about reflective learning and looks at how it can be employed in the best way to ensure your CPD benefits from it.

Obviously critical reflection plays a crucial part in CPD – being 'reflective' generally means exploring experiences and moving into new understanding, which will enable the development of practice to occur. As we saw earlier, new understanding is a key feature of a deep approach to learning, as opposed to surface learning (Marton and Säljö, 1976). We can particularly see how reflection helps to lift subconscious or informal learning to a more conscious and formalised level, using critically analytical and evaluative questions. Only such conscious learning becomes deep, meaningful and able to be owned, and thus able to impact on the development of professional judgement and expertise, and in turn enhance service quality. This book is not intending to explore reflection or reflective practice in detail. There are other texts that already do that extremely well, such as Thompson and Thompson (2008). The aim here is explore the learning involved with reflective processes and try to enhance it.

Reflective processes

To begin, Strampel and Oliver (2010) suggest the use of feedback, prompts and questions (from self and others) to encourage greater analysis and evaluation within reflective learning.

- Start with basic information and describe the event in detail (what was seen, done, heard and said?)

- Share/express emotions (what were your reactions, feelings?)

- Begin analysis of the event and how it affected you: how and why were decisions made in the way they were, things done the way they were or happened the way they did; were your thoughts, beliefs, values challenged?

- Examine reason and justification: e.g. how did you decide what to do, what influenced this?

- Explore alternatives: e.g. what else might have been going on; what other explanations, interpretations, ways of seeing this are there; what other things might you have thought/ considered/done? This section will benefit greatly from the input of others' ideas!

- Try to evaluate what happened: is there anything you'd like to take forward for the future, or do differently? Why?

- Look to the future and your professional growth: how can this change be achieved, what plans or actions need to be undertaken?

- Reconsider your ideas: how has any new understanding impacted on your personal beliefs and understandings about practice or this group of people?

We can perhaps extend this list ourselves. For example, I would add a more explicit point about needing to explore and examine what went really well too.

As Ikuenobe (2001) points out, reflective questions can seek to clarify and analyse issues and concepts, and they can help someone unearth tacit knowledge or unpack complex and implicit meaning. In addition, of course, questions, 'whether they are aiming to seek further information or provoke critical analysis are not asked in a vacuum' (333). They also operate within the context of background assumptions and beliefs which need to be questioned as well. For example, we will not have the right attitude to learning if we think it involves knowing the one correct answer to a question, or that certain types of knowledge represent a type of absolute truth that cannot be questioned. This links us back to the discussion in Chapter 3 about approaches to knowledge and learning, and we will explore these ideas further when we look at levels of criticality later in this chapter too.

Concerns with reflection

Falseness

There are a number of difficulties associated with reflection and learning, as I am sure you are aware. There is a particular 'falseness' in doing it, especially for purposes of progression and development. We may understand that it does not need to be a representation of perfect practice, but we are also aware that it has to meet particular requirements and so we will say what others need to hear. This may not be a totally accurate report of what went on at the time. Reflection is not foolproof in any case. Remembering the past is dependent on many different factors and is fallible. When an experience is reflected on, the original event becomes shaped and coloured by that reflection.

Getting the balance right can be difficult, especially if you are unsure of what is required at any particular time. Undertaking reflection is about embodying the nature and values of a profession, such as when you become a care manager, rather than just knowing something about it or going through the motions of doing it. However, your disposition at work and the approaches you take to work situations (the quality associated with your practice) will be so closely tied in with your personality and previous history that a truly honest reflective examination can be very difficult to achieve.

Negativity

As we know reflection can become very negative and particularly destructive unless it is also strengths-based (Rutter and Brown, 2011). Questioning can be considered a way of 'casting aspersions on one's ability or the reasonableness of one's view' and 'tends to engender a defensive response' (Ikuenobe, 2001: 325). By questioning we open things up, with the result that the things we knew may prove to be false. We all have an investment in our beliefs and understandings, and if they are shown to be flawed or unjustifiable, it can be a huge loss to us. At the other end of the scale, reflection can also become self-justifying and self-serving leading to a position of 'I reflect therefore I am OK!'. Placing ourselves at the centre of an event or experience can lead to a preoccupation that can border on self-absorption, and so reflection can produce unrealistic and untested delusions of expertise.

Elusiveness

Reflecting on the scope of any work being undertaken – the skills, methods, tasks, and so on – may be relatively more easy than on the quality of the work being undertaken, for reasons highlighted earlier about its lack of clarity. Being reflective may not always determine or clarify the intuitive, moral and practical reasoning processes being reflected on. The nuances of practice are by nature extremely tacit (Schön, 2001). Reflection-on-action has also been criticised for becoming overly mechanistic, too removed from practice, focused only on theory–practice integration or just not critical enough (Rutter, 2012; Bradbury *et al.*, 2010). In essence, Clegg (2009: 411) notes that the literature on reflection, although extensive, does not actually provide an 'account of the internal conversation such reflection presumes'; nor does it define its collective and social processes regarding the involvement of others. In conclusion, there is 'considerable confusion' among practitioners about 'what reflective practice entails' (Thompson and Pascal, 2012: 311).

Need for reflexivity

Wick *et al.* (2010) highlight a number of associated problematic areas. As reflective questioning can create anxiety, it will not help those who do not have the courage to admit errors or enough emotional intelligence to be that self-knowing. People will use defensive reasoning and seek plausibility rather than accuracy, and aim to preserve the status quo. Reflection's requirement to actively seek information which sheds doubt on assumptions is hard to achieve, especially if we are feeling vulnerable because of our lack of experience or we are working within an oppressive working culture (O'Sullivan, 2011). In these circumstances, we will tend to gather evidence to back up initial thoughts and feelings. Our gut feeling can influence the kind of evidence we look for, so that theory and research or other evidence will be used to back up our initial opinions (Collins and Daly, 2011). This is known as confirmation bias, the tendency to persist in initial judgements and re-frame, minimise or dismiss any new evidence that does not align with them.

Other writers highlight how extremely difficult it is to fully recognise the influences on practice. For example, Taylor and White (2000, 2001) show that procedures, habits, rules and routines can constantly suppress our positive emotional responses, such as compassion. White (2009: 230) also notes that because we had emotions before we had language, reasoning will naturally follow any moral judgement to justify it, rather than lead it. Moral judgement is by nature unconscious and concealed from us, and so our reasoning can easily be an afterthought to judgements which were made on other grounds. The effect of team talk (a group's normative or standardised understandings about a client group), and of theories which have been popularised so much that they are now skewed and misleading, are noted by these authors as additional significant but hidden influences which will automatically, but unconsciously, affect our interpretation of clients' behaviours.

Reflection, therefore, can easily produce a convenient repackaging of intuitive or biased professional judgement. In order for significant and meaningful learning to emerge, a high level of reflexivity and courage is necessary, to acknowledge and actively explore these influences: the effect emotion has on us, the licence we give ourselves to justify our moral judgements, and the language and the descriptions we use in practice.

Improving reflective learning

To try to alleviate some of these issues and ensure your reflection enhances learning as much and as positively as possible, a number of strategies can be adopted.

Focus on learning objectives

Directionless reflection is not very useful for CPD. It is best to have a particular aim and focus. Undertaking CPD within the process outlined in Chapter 2, or any other scheme that has created learning objectives, will help target thoughts and also produce useful explicit outcomes. You will be reflecting on something fairly concrete and be more aware of the level of your thinking and the progress you are making.

Involve others

As we have seen, useful activities to try to enable reflection to be as meaningful as it can be include sharing thoughts with, and being questioned by, others, especially if they are skilled in using critical questioning techniques. This is why group work and discussion with supervisors, mentors, colleagues and fellow students is particularly important for most CPD situations (so long as the learning environment is safe and supportive). Other people can help ensure you are analysing and evaluating your thinking and actions in the best way; if they are critical reflectors themselves, they will immediately pick up on any convenient glossing over or economies of truth. They can also help your reflection to turn outwards as well, onto practice values, principles, traditions and the wider context relevant to the issue. In fact, prompted conscious critical thinking with skilled others underpins the best type of reflection for meaningful analysis and refinement of practice (Otienoh, 2011). It will enable you to experience other worldviews, see things in different contexts, have a better chance to become aware of and challenge your assumptions, and to develop and use your new understanding (Brockbank and McGill, 2002).

There are a number of cautions here. One is that critical questioning does involve very skilful framing of insightful and empathetic questions to encourage analysis and challenge thinking. As was noted in Williams and Rutter (2010), this is a skill which may require training, and we suggested that facilitators need to be aware of the effect questioning has on others and to watch for any negative signs, such as non-response, a defensive position being argued too aggressively, brooding resignation. Many skills may be transferred from the type of work undertaken already with service users, of course, and Brookfield (1987: 93–4) suggests the following general guidelines:

- be specific – relate questions to particular events, situations, people and actions;
- work from the particular to the general – exploring a general theme within the context of a specific event helps people feel they are in familiar territory;
- be conversational – informal non-threatening tones help people feel comfortable.

Anyone enabling others or creating learning environments for reflection, or being enabled themselves, needs to recognise that the key is not to focus on 'answers', but instead focus on the reasoning needed to think through some answers. Linking again to our previous discussions about approaches to knowledge, if we are confronted only with established knowledge and set answers, we will be led towards absolutist thinking; if confronted by multiple viewpoints without critical examination of their relative merits, we will be led to multiplist thinking. To be enabled to undertake the most appropriate thinking for learning from reflection – contextual thinking – we need to be confronted by the need to weigh up complex evidence and experience explicit and reasoned judgement-making (Golding, 2011).

Even so, emotions are still an integral part of learning, and because the unlearning, destabilisation and disorientation which may result from critical reflection has the potential to provoke insecurity and anxiety, learning can truly benefit from the support of others and a positive learning environment and culture. Strampel and Oliver (2010) argue that it is necessary to ensure you have at least one safe opportunity for collaborative learning, either through supervision, mentorship, coaching or informal contact with colleagues. They see that it is necessary to scrutinise and analyse emotions, whether they are anxieties, fears or excitement, and to be helped to see the connections and influences between them and later decisions or actions. It is part of understanding of how difficulties and successes are coped with on a personal level.

The need for humility as well as honesty is perhaps a key point here too. It especially holds true if you are working in a partnership of trust with other staff. You have to model reflective behaviour in order to be credible, but the extra awareness that humility can bring to the process may help address some of the power issues between managers/leaders and others; for example, it may enhance sensitivity towards another person's perspective.

Be aware of levels of criticality

Being aware of the different levels of criticality and critical thought within any reflective learning process is useful. In the model devised by Argyris and Schön (1974) for organisational learning, for example, learning involves the detection and correction of error and can be undertaken at a number of critical levels. An initial and usual response to something that goes wrong is to assume that it is the wrong strategy and adopt another one – they call this *single-loop learning*. This is because the alternative strategy chosen will be implemented within the existing variables (the same goals, values, plans, frameworks, rules). However, single loop learning is unlikely to identify any underlying errors within those variables, because they have been accepted and left unexamined. The next level of learning, then, is to reflect on and question these existing variables and any other assumptions, and alter them. There is now a shift in the way a new strategy is essentially framed, which will produce a range of alternative ideas about it. This is *double-loop learning*. These authors argue that double-loop learning is necessary if practitioners are to make informed decisions in rapidly changing and often uncertain contexts. This learning should also encompass and, if possible, inform policy changes at the organisational level where appropriate. *Triple-loop learning* takes the approach even further, to examine, reflect on and question how the variables are formed in the first place. We can explore this further with an activity.

ACTIVITY 4.1

Critical levels within reflective learning

Decide on a recent example of practice where you were following a procedure, and use the table below to start unpicking and examining what you did at each of the three levels (or loops).

Single loop	*Focus on actions and procedures and accepting standard practices. The questions can be answered by yes or no. It is about right or wrong ways to do things and leads to incremental learning.*	*Ask questions such as: Am I doing things right? Did I do this the right way? Did I follow procedures? Am I undertaking them correctly and following the rules?*
Double loop	*Focus on assumptions and alternatives underlying the standard procedures and processes. This leads to reframing the issue and more options. It is about finding a different way to explain what is happening.*	*Ask questions such as: Am I doing the right things? Was the approach the right one in the first place? What different things could I have done? Do the rules need changing?* *Have I got the right information; have I involved/consulted the right people?*
Triple loop	*Focus on questioning the cultures, values and the hidden 'givens' in a situation. This leads to transformational shifts in seeing more clearly what our position is, based on questioning its rationale.*	*Ask questions such as: How do I/we 'decide' what is the 'right' information, or people, or outcomes etc.?* *How do I/we think about and make decisions on the rules; how are they made?* *What are my own or the organisation's underlying norms, cultures, policies and objectives based on? Do they need rethinking or modifying?*

Gray's (2007) analysis of this topic presents another way of looking at these three levels:

- reflection – examining the justification for one's beliefs;

- critical reflection – making an assessment of the validity of one's assumptions (examining both their sources and consequences) on personal and social levels;

- critical reflexivity – reassessing the way one has posed problems and one's orientation to perceiving, believing and acting.

Ways forward

In effect, reflection for CPD can be difficult and humbling, but the new situation gained should be pleasurable; better knowing should be appreciated. It is Ikuenobe (2001) who perhaps points out the bottom line here. It may be superficially more comfortable to remain unquestioned and unchallenged but it is not ultimately rewarding or satisfying. Our notion of professionalism and capability means that a view has to be taken that sees reflective questioning as necessary for critical thinking and good practice. He explains that taking this view is the mark of someone who is always willing to learn, because he or she realises and accepts that as humans we are fallible and liable to make mistakes. There is an ongoing awareness of the need to ensure our views and understandings are reasonable and justified and to adopt a rigorous and critical attitude to evaluating our statements, beliefs, perceptions, reasoning and arguments, as well as any form of evidence.

Another significant point here is that achieving the necessary level and depth of reflection to ensure meaningful learning for CPD is not only dependent upon a person's disposition to undertake it, but also depends to a large extent on a context that allows for and supports reflection in the same way. Many managerialist workplace cultures will not promote the openness and flexibility required here, because they believe in the use of rules and procedure to reduce it and ensure good practice through compliance instead. If you work in such a culture, you will need to think through and deal with this in a way that you feel comfortable with but which also allows your professionalism to remain intact. As seen above, actively seeking out alternative opportunities, contacts and safe spaces to create your own more conducive learning environment may be the best way forward. It may help to develop a learning culture in a wider sense for others in the workplace too. If you are in a managerial or leadership position, there may be a level of responsibility within your role to do this. Some of these ideas are developed further in the following chapter.

FURTHER READING

Fook, J. and Gardner, F. (2007) *Practising Critical Reflection: A Handbook*. Maidenhead: McGraw Hill/OU Press.

Knott, C. and Scragg, T. (2007) *Reflective Practice in Social Work*. Exeter: Learning Matters.

Thompson, S. and Thompson, N. (2008) *The Critically Reflective Practitioner*. Basingstoke: Palgrave Macmillan.

Chapter 5

Learning environments for CPD

In this chapter, the most appropriate learning environments for CPD are explored (learning cultures and communities of practice) as well as the roles of people in the workplace. It is not only managers and supervisors who become involved here – colleagues and the people who use services also have particular parts to play in your learning.

Of course, any individual should not be expected to carry the entire burden of undertaking CPD alone, and the onus for undertaking CPD is acknowledged as a partnership of equal responsibility between the individual and the organisation (Skills for Care in SWRB, 2010). Employers obviously have a crucial role in facilitating CPD through the management of training and development, and they are expected to provide opportunities for ongoing learning and development by the Social Work Task Force (SWTF, 2009). The Standards for Employers and Supervision Framework held by the Local Government Association (**www.education.gov.uk/swrb/employers**) applies to all social work employers and specifies minimum requirements, such as having access to regular quality supervision from a qualified registered social worker. Again, it is advisable to check these and The College's website for up-to-date information.

My own experience has shown that the active support of employers and managers is very important in enabling practitioners to complete CPD programmes successfully. Research also shows that formal training is most effective when delivered in conjunction with in-house mentoring and real workload relief (Doel *et al.*, 2008). This can be achieved via the provision and interlinking of formal training/staff development and the encouragement and support of informal learning cultures. O'Sullivan (2006: 11) says CPD should be '. . . managed on a continuing basis through the promotion of learning as an integral component of work, introducing a culture of learning' rather than disconnected 'injections of training', ensuring clear strategies to guide the integration between learning and work.

Blewett advocates manageable workloads and for social workers to be:

> provided with sophisticated developmental opportunities that include access to post-qualifying courses, high quality and coherent internal training programmes and reflective professional supervision.

> (2011: 191)

Staff development

The formal systems and tools associated with CPD include:

- performance appraisal;
- planned training and development events such as workshops or e-learning packages;
- mentoring;
- supervision;
- portfolio-keeping for professional registration requirements.

In most cases, CPD is identified within supervision and an appraisal framework, with a personal development plan linked to organisational goals. As Skills for Care (SWRB, 2010: 3) states, CPD planning is also part of the wider workforce planning process and should 'be a negotiated plan that satisfies both individual and organisational needs'. Such a plan is best developed, monitored and reviewed as part of ongoing performance management arrangements which involve:

- an annual cycle of objective-setting and appraisal;
- learning and development planning and review;
- a formal mid-year review/update integrated within regular supervision meetings.

Managers and other appropriate people are therefore expected to:

- help agree learning needs and objectives;
- ensure access to or supply of suitable learning opportunities;
- use supervision or other appropriate methods to discuss progress, to support reflection on experiences and enable meaningful use and evaluation of learning in practice.

Supervision

Supervision has always been seen as pivotal for good practice and CPD. It has been widely written about throughout the years, with most of the literature identifying the following four key functions:

- management – allocating and monitoring work, ensuring quality of practice;
- support – providing pastoral care for the individual (not counselling);
- education – providing support for professional development;
- mediation – balancing the needs of the individual supervisee with the needs of the organisation. Providing a channel for two-way information flow.

As mentioned earlier, the importance of the educational function for professionals working in today's complex and rapidly changing society has been particularly highlighted in recent recommendations. The Standards for Employers and Supervision Framework (**www.education. gov.uk/swrb/employers**) outlines the following four key elements which must be provided in supervision for social workers:

- improve the quality of decision-making and interventions;

- enable effective line management and organisational accountability;

- identify and address issues related to caseloads and workload management;

- help to identify and achieve further personal learning, career and development opportunities.

The guidance that forms part of this supervision framework makes it clear that if you are a social worker you should be supported to make quality decisions and interventions, by space being created in supervision for critical reflection. This should include reflection on how practice can be improved and how barriers to effective working can be minimised, to develop capacity to use your experiences to review your practice, receive feedback on performance, build emotional resilience and think reflectively about the relationships you have formed with service users and carers. These are obviously key areas for CPD and we have already looked closely at reflective processes in the previous chapter.

Cooper notes that a learning partnership approach to supervision is the best way to facilitate professional development and learning, though dialogue and negotiation within a range of accountabilities:

> The supervisor has an important facilitative role to play in encouraging awareness of reflexive practices and the integration of this into the practitioner's chosen route of CPD . . .
>
> (2008: 235)

Blewett (2011: 189) sees supervision as a 'less formal but nevertheless more fundamental mechanism by which the CPD needs of social workers' can be met in the workplace. For him, supervision at its best combines professional accountability with support and development. It is here that critical reflection can be prompted and modelled, and critical thinking encouraged and supported through exploring the assumptions underpinning case work.

Knowing what the supervision role should be providing for your CPD could guide you to find someone else to perform some of these tasks where necessary; you could request mentoring, or ask a critical friend or colleague to help. Or you may seek help to improve your own supervision practice. This is where learning cultures become important and influential – they are discussed later in this chapter.

It is not the intention of this book to discuss these staff development systems and tools in any detail. Other sources can be used for this, including advice from Skills for Care and The College. A number of ideas are extended within Williams *et al.* (2012), which contains sections on appraisal and supervision.

Service users and carers

We also need to recognise that service users and carers will be agents of work-based learning too (Burton and Jackson, 2006), creating the everyday experiences which shape professional judgement and practice. Their reactions and experiences provide the feedback we need to acknowledge, reflect on and work with. There are a number of ways in which service users and carers can be involved in work-based learning and enhance professional understanding and awareness, either within the practice relationship or in addition to it. Both the Social Care Institute for Excellence (SCIE) and the Social Work Education Participation (SWEP) groups share good practice about the participation of service users and carers in social work education.

As so much learning takes place through informal and experiential ways, the more that can be viewed through a service user's or carer's perspective, the more learning and development should take place. A recent and relatively unexplored area of service user participation is to involve service users and carers more directly and equally in supporting reflective practice. Hafford-Letchfield *et al.* (2008) suggest establishing methods and systems for users' involvement such as group supervision session, non-managerial support, mentoring, and opportunities to explore the material contained within reflective diaries or learning journals. (The service users would obviously need to fully respect confidentiality and not work with individual or teams who are involved in their care.) They suggest the creation of safe spaces for exploring any fears associated with the idea of involving users in supporting reflective practice, explaining that there is as much to learn from:

> *exploring the perceived barriers and power dynamics associated with users facilitating reflective learning as there will be from actually reflecting on practice.*

> (2008: 91)

ACTIVITY 5.1

Users of services supporting reflective practice

Reflect on how you or your colleagues would feel about being mentored or supported by service users and/or their carers. In which circumstances would such involvement be appropriate or not; why?

Does this shift in roles seem threatening or uncomfortable? As a potential barrier to learning, how could these feeling be approached or dealt with?

Learning cultures

The Social Work Reform Board (SWRB, 2010) emphasises the importance of determining and creating the right environment for the professional learning and development of others. An emphasis on creating a learning culture within organisations is particularly noted by the Munro Review, with suggestions for creating an approach that values 'professional social work expertise' and a learning culture 'where expert professional judgement is the mainstay' (Munro, 2011: 9–10).

The significance and importance of the wider community especially needs to be fully recognised. In fact, it is an organisation's or a team's culture of learning which can determine whether CPD is undertaken in a meaningful and successful way. In their report, the SWRB (2010) acknowledge the responsibility an organisation has for developing and actively supporting a strong learning culture. The Munro Review (2011) goes further by understanding that the more usual and dominant culture of compliance in any organisation needs to be dealt with first before a more conducive learning culture can be achieved. It recommends:

[a] radical reduction in the amount of central prescription to help professionals move from a compliance culture to a learning culture, where they have more freedom to use their expertise in assessing need and providing the right help.

(2011: 6–7)

Emotion

The role of emotion is significant here. CPD can prove lonely and also sometimes anxiety provoking or threatening, and therefore needs to be supported and enabled in empowering work-based relationships and partnerships, that is, genuine learning cultures. There is an 'interplay of interest, anxiety, and excitement from which a feeling of safety, which is fundamental for learning', should evolve, 'creating a resilience and readiness for learning' (Claxton, 1999, cited in Simons and Ruijters, 2001: 18). It not only requires your commitment and dedication in order to persevere, it also requires recognition, value, encouragement and support from others around you. Munro (2011) recognises that a better understanding of the nature of health and social care practice is required here, which acknowledges the emotional dimensions and intellectual nuances of professional reasoning and judgement. These need to be valued, shared and developed within and across organisations to enable high quality services. Allowing professionals greater opportunity for responsible innovation and space for professional judgement, therefore, seems a fundamental principle for any learning organisation.

Some of you may be fortunate enough to work in a positive learning culture which encourages sharing of knowledge, plus feedback and evaluation of services. Others, however, will be operating in a culture of fear in the current risk-focused environment, and so any analysis or reflection on practice is likely to become merely describing and justifying the bases for decisions rather than exploring them. CPD becomes reduced to 'covering your back' rather than learning to develop and trust your judgement. In this situation, as noted earlier, more private and safer opportunities will need to be sought where you, or others you trust, can ask supportive critical questions of your practice that aim for clarification, deeper thinking and a review of your reasoning and judgements (Collins and Daly, 2011).

Contribution

It is important to note that all individuals are able, and have a responsibility, to contribute to a learning culture and a positive learning environment (i.e. not just managers, leaders or work-based educators). This can be done by maximising and improving informal practice-based learning or opportunities for it.

For example, basic adult learning principles (Knowles, 1980) could be adhered to when learning in a group or in a team environment.

- Help promote conditions that foster deep learning and professional capability by questioning where appropriate.

- Display self-awareness, emotional intelligence.

- Be open to others, to experiences, to feedback.

- Avoid telling or offering solutions which create dependency – do not provide answers but assist others to find answers themselves.

- Encourage others to join in and share thoughts/feelings/ideas.

- Recognise individuals' capabilities and needs.

Whether you are undertaking CPD yourself or enabling others, it is about working with people: becoming aware of and bringing out the best in others and yourself. For example, a discussion about the latest training with others can help lift it from a surface learning to a deeper learning event, as different ideas start to be considered on how to realistically integrate it in practice. To that end, everyone learns and gains something, leading to collective and shared outcomes such as insights, different perspectives, innovations, action plans. It is important to develop contacts with other people to help with learning because the social aspect to learning, especially self-managed learning (although this sounds paradoxical), is essential. This is not only about support – it is how others can help you develop or consider different perspectives by sharing their own ideas and prompting your deeper thinking.

For McArdle and Coutts (2010), CPD is seen as shared 'sense-making' and collaborative action within communities of practice. Lave and Wenger (1991: 98) originally note that a community of practice involves participants who are united in action as well as in the meaning of that action. The community tends to be held together by its joint enterprise and shared purpose. Of course, some communities may become restrictive or sustain unacceptable practice, and so ground rules and values need to be constantly monitored. In essence, though, a good community of practice provides a safe and supportive learning environment and therefore embeds an effective culture of learning for CPD. It does not necessarily need formal managerial input, but it will benefit from being managed appropriately by practitioners themselves (Gray *et al.*, 2010).

In other words, CPD can be enhanced by anyone by undertaking or modelling it in a certain way so that the learning is uncovered and shared in a productive and supportive environment. If you are specifically aiming to support or enable the CPD of others, it would be useful to refer to other texts in this series, such as Williams and Rutter's (2010) *The Practice Educator's Handbook*, which deal with this area of practice in much more detail.

ACTIVITY 5.2

Your learning environment

Note where your risk-free safe opportunities are for:

- *emotional support;*

- *discussing different perspectives;*

- *critical questioning and challenge;*

- *exploring alternative approaches, ideas, outcomes;*

- *fully exploring how you deal with complexity, risk, uncertainty;*

- *making new theory–practice connections;*

- *feedback.*

FURTHER READING

Kadushin, A. and Harkness, D. (2002) *Supervision in Social Work*, 4th edn. New York: Columbia University Press.

Thompson, N. (2006) *Promoting Workplace Learning*. Bristol: Policy Press.

Tyler, G. (2006) Addressing barriers to participation: Service user involvement in social work training. *Social Work Education*, 25(4): 385–92.

Wenger, E. (2000) Communities of practice and social learning systems. *Organisation*, 2: 225–46.

Chapter 6
Assessing CPD learning output

As we have seen, learning for CPD can take place in a number of different ways, and the considerable amount of informal learning in social work and health care that takes place needs to be secured as an opportunity to gain recognition and credit for CPD. As is noted throughout the book, in an outcomes approach, the emphasis is on what difference learning has made rather than what learning was undertaken. The assessing and formal accreditation of CPD is therefore a crucially important consideration when determining the level of learning that has occurred and the impact it has had on us as individuals, our professional practice and the service itself. This chapter explores a number of frameworks that can help you determine and assess professional development, in particular the PCF.

Appropriate frameworks should allow practitioners to gauge the impact of their learning on their professional development: the changes in thinking and behaviour, and the subsequent transformation in practice at a service level. Therefore, an aligned system for accreditation and assessment of CPD is required that can define specific levels of professional thinking and behaviour in order to take account not only of the scope of work being undertaken and enhanced, but also the quality of that work. Professional capability, as hard as it is to define, has to be included but not over-specified.

Collins and Daly (2011: 24) show that assessment frameworks can be useful for reminding practitioners of what are 'good enough' levels for assessing judgement. Obviously the quality of judgement here rests on how high the level of 'good enough' is set. Nevertheless, assessment frameworks will not be able to give explicit guidance for specific instances or situations. Best use of them will always rely on sufficient professional understanding and judgement to interpret them and their standards or criteria appropriately. If this is achieved then the quality of that practice should be able to be appraised in a reliable and robust manner.

Evidence for output and impact

A number of items are referred to as potential sources of evidence in recent advice from The College on assessing work-based learning using the PCF:

- critical reflection outputs (e.g. Critical Incident Analysis);
- direct observation;
- supervision records;
- service user feedback.

As stated earlier, evidence from your practice experience is fully valid if it demonstrates and evaluates your professional reasoning, decision-making and actions for those situations. It is not valid if it consists of anecdotes and only describes what you did or thought, or if it tries to make wider or more generalised assertions.

Frameworks for determining and assessing change and development

We can look at a number of ways in which the development of practice has been categorised by others in a range of frameworks below. We start with the PCF and look at its use in some detail. These ideas may help you to define the impact and output of your learning, or that of others, for assessment purposes. If you are using the CPD cycle explained in Chapter 2, it is important to refer back to the original learning outcomes and evaluate progress against these as well. The impact on oneself, on practice and on service quality should be made explicit and evaluated carefully, so that organisations and employers can also appreciate what your learning has achieved.

(1) The Professional Capabilities Framework (PCF)

As noted in Chapter 2, the PCF shows the range of capabilities being covered as domains (e.g. knowledge, intervention and skills) but also the transition points between the various professional levels for social workers. Use of these PCF levels should help with defining the scope of practice and particular areas of capability or the quality of practice, where development is being aimed for. For progression and career development purposes, the output of CPD should relate to the specific guidance contained within the PCF fan diagram (**www.collegeofsocialwork.org/pcf.aspx**). This includes details of the different levels or roles (qualifying; assessed and supported year in practice; social worker; experienced social worker; advanced practitioner; principal social worker) within each domain. These levels are also aligned to the relevant HCPC Standards of Conduct, Performance, and Ethics; Standards of Proficiency and Standards of CPD (**www.hcpc-uk.org**); and the Quality Assurance Agency (QAA) subject benchmark statement for social work (**www.qaa.ac.uk/**).

Table 6.1 looks in more detail at an example of the capability domain for professional leadership and at two levels within it.

Obviously, it is important to note the roles and tasks associated with each level when aiming for progression, and use them to help you clarify and assess the output and impact of CPD. Some of them, because they deal with the quality of practice or the more elusive aspects of it, will be vague (e.g. 'promote a culture of professional curiosity'). It will therefore be necessary to explore these in groups, or in appropriate one-to-one situations, to ensure there is a shared understanding of what this could entail. As we saw earlier, this can be a very empowering and necessary part of practice which allows you to determine your professionalism and capability.

The College is particularly keen, also, to see the notion of 'holistic assessment' being adhered to here in order to avoid an 'unquestioning adherence to demonstrating progression by presenting specific instances of meeting a particular bullet point' (TCSW, 2012). It explains that the nine capabilities should be seen as interdependent; they interact in professional practice,

Table 6.1 Example of a PCF capability domain and two levels

Example of a PCF capability domain and two levels

Capability: Professional Leadership

The social work profession evolves through the contribution of its members in activities such as practice research, supervision, assessment of practice, teaching and management. An individual's contribution will gain influence when undertaken as part of a learning, practice-focused organisation. Learning may be facilitated with a wide range of people including social work colleagues, service users and carers, volunteers, foster carers and other professionals.

Level: Experienced Social Worker

- Contribute to organisational developments.
- Play leading role in practice development in the team and help sustain a learning culture.
- Provide supervision to colleagues as organisation determines. Support others to manage and prioritise work.
- Assess and manage the work of social work students and Assessed and Supported Year in Employment (ASYE).
- Practice Educator Standards Stage 2: Domain B and C (see also capability 1).

Level: Advanced Practitioner

- Ensure individual and organisational practice is informed by current research and knowledge.
- Promote, articulate and support a positive social work identity.
- Promote a culture of professional curiosity.

Taken from the interactive PCF Fan Diagram. The College of Social Work.
Available from: **www.collegeofsocialwork.org/pcf.aspx**

with the result that many issues will be relevant to more than one capability. For The College, the focus within practice learning needs to move from the collection of pieces of evidence towards assessment of professional capability. Using work by Biggs (2007), they show that a holistic decision about the quality of performance is arrived at by understanding the whole in the light of the parts, that is, the integrated action, not the performance of any one part (although this does not mean that the detail of the parts is ignored).

The College's paper on understanding holistic assessment (TCSW, 2012) notes that the individual capability statements are important for providing the detail for the expectations within each domain. They can be used to identify gaps, areas of development or concerns. However, it also suggests starting with an overall judgement backed up by reference to all nine domains, which will better reflect the nature of holistic assessment. Therefore, when working with the PCF to evaluate or assess your development, or that of others, it is important to look across all the domains and refer to them in order to ascertain a complete picture of practice, but also to highlight more specific elements within a domain that help identify the particular areas where progression can be seen in detail. Material developed by The College will be able to help with this type of 'mapping'.

At the time of writing, version 1 of the paper on holistic assessment (TCSW, 2012) sets out the initial principles for holistic assessment for the Assessed and Supported Year in Employment, but further guidance will be developed later by The College. It does contain some more general principles, though, which apply to assessment across the whole of the PCF.

1. Assessment is progressive over a period of time (e.g. initial qualifying placement, ASYE), leading to effective summative assessment.

2. Assessment must be consistent with the appropriate PCF level descriptor, and include sufficiency and depth of evidence across all nine domains.

3. Individual capability statements will be important in terms of providing detail of expectations for each domain, and particularly significant to identify gaps, areas of development or concerns.

4. The assessment process and judgement must be trustworthy, reliable and transparent (e.g. include clear guidance in handbooks, assessment panels, triangulated evidence, audit trails).

5. Evidence must include the ability to reflect critically, including reference to different sources of knowledge and research.

6. The learner will contribute evidence for assessment but the professional judgement of sufficiency must be made by a registered social worker. (At initial qualifying level, assessors must meet the Practice Educator Professional Standards.)

Further draft guidance, templates and exemplars of best practice that can support and enable holistic assessment supported by evidence will be made available through The College's website. The College's online portfolio can also help, as it will contain pre-formed headings or questions that provide focus and guide direction.

(2) The Components of Expertise (Atherton, 2011)

In Atherton's model, there is a base of *competence* which he describes as the simple ability to perform the requisite range of skills for practice – knowing what to do. Although we may question his use of the word competence, an initial level of basic understanding is still relevant. His next level is *contextualisation*, which is about knowing when to do what. He explains that this level contains the additional skill of flexibility, discrimination and discretion, which enables a practitioner to select the appropriate method for the situation. Further on there is a *contingency* level, where there is a greater flexibility to be able to cope when things go wrong. It implies a great depth of understanding of the situation, which can be drawn upon to develop a strategy for action which does not simply rely on predetermined procedures. The element of strategy becomes more explicit here. Finally there is *creativity*, which is the capacity to use all the 'lower' level skills in new ways to solve new problems. In this model it is strategic thinking that grows in importance, and progression is seen to be an ability to become aware of possibilities and develop plans to deal with them.

These levels may prove useful to identify and categorise the more holistic levels of progression and confidence which you are achieving; plus, for areas of leadership or management, the level of strategic thinking you are attaining.

(3) Dreyfus and Dreyfus skill acquisition model

This model identifies five stages in the development of expertise through which a learner advances: novice, advanced beginner, competent, proficient and expert (see Table 6.2). The learner progresses through the five stages, starting from detached, abstract and consciously analytic behaviour in a situation to more involved, skilled behaviour which is based on unconscious and intuitive recognition of similarities and patterns.

This model was extended and enhanced by Fook *et al.*'s (2000) *expertise model,* which presents a theory on how social work expertise is learned and developed. Their seven-stage model identifies eleven dimensions specifically developed for complex practice and decision-making. These dimensions consist of: substantive knowledge, procedural knowledge, skills, values, contextuality, reflexivity, breadth of vision, flexibility, use of theory, approach, and perspective on profession.

These levels may prove useful to identify and categorise the type of expert thinking you are achieving.

Table 6.2 Dreyfus and Dreyfus (1986) skill acquisition model

1.	Novice	Rigid adherence to taught rules or plans. Little situational perception. No discretionary judgement.
2.	Advanced beginner	Guidelines for action based on attributes or aspects. Situational perception still limited. All attributes and aspects are treated separately and given equal importance.
3.	Competent	Coping with 'crowdedness'. Now sees actions at least partly in terms of longer-term goals. Conscious deliberate planning. Standardised and routinised procedures.
4.	Proficient	Sees situations holistically rather than in terms of aspects. Sees what is most important in a situation. Perceives deviations from the normal pattern. Decision-making less laboured. Uses maxims (rules) for guidance, whose meaning varies according to the situation.
5.	Expert	No longer relies on rules, guidelines or maxims. Intuitive grasp of situations based on deep tacit understanding. Analytic approaches used only in novel situations or when problems occur. Vision of what is possible.

(4) Conscious competence learning model

Material adapted from Atherton (2011), the **www.businessballs.com** website and Williams and Rutter (2010).

The model appears to have been initially developed at Gordon Training International in the 1970s. It shows four stages associated with learning new skills. It can be used in any number of ways to support learning, as a useful reminder of the fact that we learn in stages, but also to recognise and articulate our own progression when learning something new.

1. Unconscious incompetence

   This is the 'ignorance is bliss' state where we do not know what we do not know. Making us aware of our ignorance will probably create anxiety, but it is an important stage in developing motivation. However, if we have a vested interest in not doing certain things or in doing things only in a particular way, this will also involve a stage of 'unlearning'.

2. Conscious incompetence

   We are aware of what we don't know. This should prompt greater motivation towards finding out more, but only if what needs to be learnt is seen as relevant and useful and other resources or support are available.

3. Conscious competence

   We are aware of what we do know. In many circumstances after learning has taken place this stage may be perfectly adequate, at least for a time. For some skills, especially advanced ones, we can regress to previous stages if we fail to practise and exercise them.

4. Unconscious competence

   We can use our knowledge without thinking about it. For example, this easily applies to practical skills such as driving or swimming, the kinds of activities we can do without thinking. However, this can also refer to a situation where we know something but do not know how we know it and probably cannot express it, such as our more intuitive understandings and hunches or our practice wisdom. If we were asked about a good piece of practice, our answer would probably fail to do justice to the complexity of what we have done.

These may prove useful to identify and categorise the levels of awareness you are achieving.

ACTIVITY 6.1

Developing expertise

Think about your development of 'expertise' in a particular situation you are now familiar with; note which aspects are now so routine or familiar to you that you can recognise them or do them almost without thinking.

Using the ideas within the last model presented above (conscious competence), make some notes on what you think a fifth level should include.

There is an interesting debate around this issue of fifth level on the **www.businessballs.com** website. At a fifth level, practitioners could use reflection or other skills to become consciously aware of what unconscious or sub-conscious abilities they are using and be able to analyse, adapt and enhance their activity.

(5) Regulatory and professional standards

A number of government, quasi-government and professional organisations produce their own sets of standards for regulatory and standardisation use within health and social care. As seen in Chapter 2, they can prove useful in helping specify the content of learning objectives for CPD, and so of course they also prove useful in helping to articulate the impact of CPD on practice and service quality – for yourself and for use with other staff. A selection of them is summarised here.

1. *The NHS Leadership Framework Overview* (see Appendix 2 for further details)

   The Leadership Framework aims to provide a consistent approach to leadership development for all staff in health and care and to represent a foundation in leadership behaviour.

   Domains and elements

   a. Demonstrating personal qualities

   b. Working with others

   c. Managing services

   d. Improving services

   e. Setting direction

   f. Creating the vision

   g. Delivering the strategy

   Available from: **www.leadershipacademy.nhs.uk/develop-your-leadership-skills/leadership-framework/the-framework-overview**

2. *Minimum training standards and code of conduct for adult social care workers and healthcare support workers in England*

- Skills for Care and Skills for Health have been commissioned by the Department of Health to jointly undertake this project. At the time of writing these areas are being consulted on and developed;

- adult social care workers (working in support of health and social care professionals, independently, for Care Quality Commission (CQC) registered residential care providers, or as domiciliary care workers in England);

- healthcare support workers (reporting to registered nurses and midwives).

The expectation is that the output from this work will be used by one or more bodies to establish voluntary registers for healthcare support workers and adult social care workers in England, as part of its standards for inclusion on a register. It aims to produce:

- a framework of core competences needed by individuals working as health and care support workers;

- a framework of technical competences required to undertake more specialised functions required by health and care support workers, which would be applicable to the context of their work setting and which would be delegated by health and social care professionals;

- a Code of Conduct for health and care support workers;

- a definition of minimum core content for induction of health and care support workers;

- reference to qualifications contained within competence frameworks to identify the links between the core and technical competence requirements and the competence-based qualifications in the QCF.

Taken from Skills for Care website. Available from: **www.skillsforcare.org.uk/qualifications_ and_training**

3. *Management Induction Standards (MIS, revised 2012)*

The MIS include core and recommended standards which Skills for Care see as valid for all those operating in a managerial role, plus some optional standards which can be adopted by managers who have those particular aspects to their role or who have a particular interest in them.

The core standards

a. Governance and accountability

b. Systems and processes to promote communication

c. Partnership working and relationships

d. Using person-centred practice to achieve positive outcomes

e. Team leadership and management

f. Managing resources

g. Equality, diversity and inclusion

h. Safeguarding and protection

The optional standards

i. Professional development

j. Change and growth

k. Managing business

l. Ensuring quality.

Skills for Care has published a booklet 'Becoming the new manager' to support the use of the MIS. It gives additional guidance for each knowledge requirement in the standards. On the Skills for Care website are a number of online templates; some are specific to the person completing the MIS and others can be used in relation to either a new manager's own CPD, or that of the workers for whom they are responsible.

Taken from Skills for Care website. Available from: **www.skillsforcare.org.uk/qualifications_ and_training**

4. *Common Induction Standards (revised 2010)*

These standards, incorporating eight key standards, are for people entering social care and those changing roles or employers within social care. They now map across to the mandatory units of the new Health and Social Care Diploma to ensure there is consistency of approach for the workforce.

- Standard 1 – Role of the health and social care worker

- Standard 2 – Personal development

- Standard 3 – Communicate effectively

- Standard 4 – Equality and inclusion

- Standard 5 – Principles for implementing duty of care

- Standard 6 – Principles of safeguarding in health and social care

- Standard 7 – Person-centred support

- Standard 8 – Health and safety in an adult social care setting

The standards provide recognition for care workers' practice and prepare them for entry into future training and qualifications. Each standard contains a number of areas of knowledge that care workers need to know about before they can work unsupervised. The Skills for Care website provides links to the revised standards with a glossary which outlines how they link to codes of practice; a progress log; a guide for those responsible for workers in an induction period; a guide for new workers; and a certificate for managers to sign to confirm that standards have been met.

Taken from Skills for Care website. Available from: **www.skillsforcare.org.uk/entry_to_ social_care**

5. *HCPC Standards of Proficiency – Social Workers in England*

The standards of proficiency (SoPs) set out what a social worker in England should know, understand and be able to do when they complete their social work training so that they can register with the HCPC. They set out clear expectations of a social worker's knowledge and abilities when they start practising. Both the PCF and the SoPs were produced at the same time and will be used by social work stakeholders. The SoPs have been mapped onto the PCF so that it can see how the two documents interact, and both the HCPC and The College websites contain the mapping documents.

Taken from the HCPC website. Available from: **www.hcpc-uk.org/publications/standards/**

Standards and criteria such as these should prove useful in identifying and evaluating the changes and development within practice for yourself and when assessing others, especially when the learning involved has not been associated with formal programmes of development. Obviously, this list is not exhaustive and there may be other professional or statutory frameworks you need to identify which may help when dealing with the impact and output of CPD.

FURTHER READING

Fook, J., Ryan, M. and Hawkins, L. (2000) *Professional Expertise: Practice, Theory and Education for Working in Uncertainty.* London: Whiting and Birch Ltd.

Parker, J. and Bradley, G. (2007) *Social Work Practice: Assessment, Planning, Intervention and Review,* 2nd edn. Exeter: Learning Matters.

Whittington, C. (2007) *Assessment in social work: a guide for learning and teaching SCIE Guide 18.* London: SCIE. Available from: **www.scie.org.uk/publications/guides/guide18/**

Chapter 7

CPD evidence for post-qualifying programmes

Recognising and assessing CPD can be made easier with the use of frameworks that show levels of progression. In universities or other academic environments, learning output is measured against specific learning outcomes associated with programme or course specifications. This chapter looks at how CPD is assessed within such environments and how work-based learning output can be aligned with academic requirements as well as the PCF. This may be necessary when undertaking PQ/CPD programmes, or for accrediting prior learning (APL). An example is provided here to illustrate how your work-based learning might be enhanced and assessed for academic purposes and incorporate the PCF too.

Post-qualifying (PQ) programmes

The PQ framework in its current form ceased to exist when the GSCC closed in July 2012, but this does not mean that PQ programmes are ending. Munro (2011: 170–1) states that it is important that higher education accredited post-qualifying courses within a national framework are not lost following the transfer of functions from the GSCC to the HCPC, because such courses play a fundamental role in the development of social work expertise. Universities will continue to offer PQ programmes with academic credit attached to them, and the new CPD framework will include opportunities to undertake modular or full PQ programmes alongside a wide range of other learning activities. The intention is for employers and higher education institutions (HEIs) to work together to meet learning and development needs.

As seen in the previous chapter, there is a need for formalised assessed programmes of learning and development which can evaluate professional thinking, reasoning and judgement. Formalised learning and assessment can provide a valid way to authenticate whether learning has taken place or not at a required level. Some would argue that the type of CPD that has the potential to improve practice and services seems to require such formalised and robust processes of engagement and measurement (Brown et al., 2012)

All training and education programmes, organisations and individuals which provide education and development for social workers are able to apply for endorsement with The College to show that they are working to an agreed set of quality criteria. The PCF, as the professional standard for social work, can underpin the work that educators and trainers undertake with social workers and their employers. The College notes that the capabilities can be used to frame the content of learning programmes as well as the teaching, learning and assessment strategies that underpin them. In effect, the learning aims and outcomes of units and modules on formalised programmes will probably be linked or mapped onto the PCF domains and levels, making it easy to show the outcomes of your learning.

Accreditation of Prior Learning (APL)

Your previous learning may be able to be used with a particular PQ programme and given accreditation. Brown *et al.* (2012) help us to explain APL in more detail here. APL refers to an academic process of assessing previous experiential or certificated learning. It allows such learning to be counted towards the completion of a programme of study (QAAHE, 2004, 2008) and results in an award of academic credit. The term accreditation refers to the process of formal acknowledgement or assessment of prior learning and achievement (QAAHE, 2004, 2008). APL is an important tool for showing the value placed on the knowledge and skills developed previously by practitioners, but it is a complex process. Most higher education institutions will have regulations about the maximum level of allowed APL credit for undergraduate and post-graduate programmes, which may prove restrictive.

For our purposes, we can say that APL is made up of two main related aspects, and they both result in academic credit or educational currency.

• Accreditation of Prior Experiential Learning (APEL)

APEL results in an award for academic credit for learning that has taken place outside formal educational institutions, that is, it is based on experience. APEL recognises the value of learning from work, community or volunteer experience not previously assessed (Cleary *et al.*, 2002; Cox and Green, 2001). A candidate often needs to submit work for assessment in a prescribed format to show they have met the learning outcomes for a particular programme or module; this may be the assessment for the programme or its equivalent and it is not an automatic process. The assessment of APEL is a challenge. The whole process can be very labour and resource intensive. APEL is just like undertaking a course or module without attending the 'teaching', but candidates still need to produce the assessment to demonstrate that learning has occurred – it is not an automatic process just because someone has been 'doing the job for years'. To provide evidence of experiential learning, candidates will need to engage in a reflective process with academic support, which may take the form of a short course or personal development planning (Johnson and Walsh, 2005). The portfolio is a common model used to assess prior experiential learning, but is not the only one.

• Accreditation of Prior Certificated Learning (APCL)

APCL allows candidates to use previously attained credit or certified learning (as opposed to experience), and 'to move between courses, or to another university, with the [academic] credits they have obtained and achieve further credits there' (HEPI, 2004: 6). A key challenge is that APCL credit transfer assumes universities are able to agree a common denomination of accounting or amount of credit for a given qualification, which does not always happen.

Partnership

A key focus here will be on the nature of any collaboration between employers and the higher education institution involved. In the context of the PCF, there is a current expectation that volumes of credit awarded for previous Specialist, Higher Specialist and Advanced level PQ awards will be able to be used by social workers as they progress through the PCF. A careful balance needs to be maintained between the needs of learners and the needs of the institutions engaged in APL activities (Cleary *et al.*, 2002).

The type of questions for collaborative partnerships to consider in addressing some of these challenges and negotiating a balance are as follows.

1. How will the APL decision-making process be made transparent, demonstrably rigorous and fair?

2. What are the limits on the amount of academic credit that can be recognised through the accreditation process?

3. What type of credit is acceptable for transfer and what is not? If particular credit is acceptable, what is its shelf-life?

4. How will accredited prior learning, certificated or experiential, be identified on students' award transcripts?

5. What is the form of assessment for the accreditation of certificated and experiential learning?

6. What training have staff undergone in relation to giving guidance on APL to prospective students?

7. How much does it cost to submit a claim for the accreditation of prior learning and how long will it take?

8. Who is the contact person for APL issues?

(Adapted from QAAHE, 2004: 7–16)

Academic use and accreditation of work-based CPD

Variation

Even though PQ programmes and any APL schemes can be mapped against the PCF, there is likely to be a degree of variance in how different academic assessment systems allow, take account of, and assess professional capability (as well as academic ability) within written work. Assessment and accreditation process and criteria should be 'fit for purpose' for CPD functions, that is, able to assess professional thinking, reasoning and arguments, but the particular written style required can vary across and also within institutions. For example, the interpretation of 'evidence-based practice' and 'theory–practice integration' can differ widely across a number of universities, and there will be difference in the degree to which a university expects you to 'back up' your professional decisions and knowledge with theory and research, or allow the first person 'I'. The expectations and requirements should be made clear but it is always worth asking for explicit clarification. The advice is to follow the specific guidance and instructions from the awarding authority when evidencing your learning and development for formal recognition or academic credit.

Alignment

This need for valid and relevant assessment of professional reasoning and judgement processes within an academic context is more important now than ever, with recent reports (e.g. Laming 2003, 2009; Munro, 2011) emphasising these processes and their associated abilities as necessary components of professional development, both individually and at an agency level (Munro, 2008). Of course, many HE programmes and APL systems can and do effectively assess work-based or reflective thinking and practices; but if you are undertaking CPD in an academic environment, or your staff are, the key questions to ask are whether:

- higher level thinking involved in professional reasoning and judgement is valued and able to be assessed in its own right using aligned criteria?;

- practice output and/or service impact is also evaluated?

The need is to ensure all aspects of professionalism are validly developed and assessed. Obviously, this is not advocating theory-less practice or a 'dumbing down' of professional education but, in order to effectively develop expertise, professionals should not be expected to rely entirely on the ideas or authority of others. We can refer back to our previous discussions on knowledge production in Chapter 3. As a professional you need to be able to discuss your development of practice and practice-based knowledge in a way that evidences its own authority (e.g. via sound critical thinking, practical reasoning, judgement and decision-making), as well as using formal knowledge to help critically inform, explain or explore the points being made. You need to be able to reason through and evaluate any type of knowledge in respect of how well it 'performs' in practice situations and then articulate the results as new understanding and as valid knowledge regarding your practice and that situation. In effect, you need to adapt and evaluate a wide range of knowledge and develop ideas of your own as a result. CPD learning in an academic environment can and should be enabling this to happen and give credit for it.

In any academic work, though, there is a distinct difference between making points regarding one's own practice and about social work practice in general. Any generalised assertions, ideas and opinions made about social work or other practice in a broader sense do require evidence from external formal sources (in the form of references to previous writers, policies, legislation, etc.) to support them.

Generic criteria

I would argue that some of the essential elements which make up good professional reasoning and judgement are the generic aspects associated with good thinking (e.g. analysis, criticality and evaluation). These elements can be used as criteria for assessing professionalism, and, indeed, they are already available as generic nationally-accepted descriptors for higher education. The UK Quality Code for Higher Education (QAAHE, 2011) details a range of qualification descriptors equally suited to critical thinking and action in a practical sense as well as an academic one. For example, at undergraduate level 6 there is requirement to:

> *critically evaluate arguments, assumptions, abstract concepts and data (that may be incomplete), to make judgements, and to frame appropriate questions to achieve a solution – or identify a range of solutions – to a problem; the exercise of initiative and personal responsibility [and] decision-making in complex and unpredictable contexts.*

(2011: 10–11)

Such descriptors easily match the professional reasoning and judgement activities detailed earlier. For more information and details, see Appendix 3. As Bourner (2003: 271–2) notes, 'the academy has a great deal of experience in detecting good critical thinking' which he argues can be a 'secure means' for assessing reflective learning and development.

Evidence from work-based learning and in-house training

As mentioned earlier, we know that much training and work-based learning is by nature only aiming for initial understanding rather than deeper thinking and engagement. When this is the case, it can be helpful to have a strategy for raising the level of learning yourself in order to utilise it more productively for CPD purposes. This becomes especially true if it is being used within an academic environment. This strategy can incorporate a CPD cycle, a deep approach to learning and an alignment with professional capability.

A series of guided activities is suggested here:

Stage 1

Explicitly develop *learning objectives* and undertake *appropriate work-based training or learning*.

Stage 2

Undertake *further reading* around the topic area to enhance critical understanding. This can extend the range and deepen understanding of relevant ideas, as well as question them.

Stage 3

Undertake a small piece of *practice-based work* to utilise the new knowledge and skills. This can allow interpretation and use of the ideas for a specific purpose.

Stage 4

Undertake *critical reflection* on impact and outcomes of this learning experience for practice and services. This can review the output from this learning on self and others.

All or some of this work can be evidenced for assessment and accreditation purposes (for academic and other CPD processes) using a portfolio consisting of your written output, which can be designed to encourage expression of professional thinking (i.e. reasoning and judgement) as well as action and critically evaluated impact.

Of course, how you choose to do this is dictated by your own circumstances and needs, but we can look in more detail at these suggested stages and use a fictional case study of Tony, an aspiring team manager, to illustrate one way each stage could be undertaken. (This case study also makes reference to particular domains in the PCF.)

Stage 1. Explicitly develop learning objectives and undertake appropriate work-based training or learning.

- Identify key learning objectives. Produce a work-based personal development/improvement plan for yourself with your line manager/appraiser or other appropriate person. A personal development plan should link to organisational goals/plans and can be an evaluation/ performance improvement plan for your practice or for the team/unit as a whole. Use could also be made of 360-degree feedback and professional benchmarks, including the PCF, to develop particular goals or objectives.

- Where appropriate arrange/attend work-based learning (i.e. training events such as in-house or other non-accredited courses, workshops or e-learning packages), undertake private study or research, or take part in specific projects to help achieve these learning objectives.

Examples of resources:

- Organisational training lists; local CDP strategies; organisational development plan/ strategies/policies.

- Relevant local and national professional sets of standards, strategies, frameworks or benchmarking tools; PCF.

CASE STUDY 7.1

Stage 1

Tony: *aspiring team manager, Children's Services, Northshire Social Service; at present undertaking the role in a colleague's absence.*

Development needs: improve my communication of strategic policy requirements to staff members – in particular, Northshire's strategy to increase levels of service user feedback and participation which can inform and have a direct impact on services provided.

Specific learning objectives (taken from his personal development plan).

- *to address problem areas in my communication skills for effective leadership/supervision . . .*

- *. . . specifically to undertake necessary staff development for improved service user feedback and participation.*

CPD areas: relating to the Professional Capabilities Framework

1 – Professionalism

6 – Critical Reflection and Analysis

9 – Professional Leadership and in particular the level of advanced practitioner

- *Ensure individual and organisational practice is informed by current research and know-ledge.*

CASE STUDY 7.1 *(CONT.)*

- *Promote, articulate and support a positive social work identity.*

- *Promote a culture of professional curiosity.*

I agreed the learning objectives, learning events and action plan with my line manager and discussed the progress I made in supervision.

The work-based learning event: in-house course on communication using neurolinguistic programming (NLP) approaches and methods.

Stage 2. Further reading around the topic area to enhance critical understanding.

Develop a wider as well as a more in-depth and critical understanding/appreciation of the subject area with further reading of published literature sources. Consider and assess the contribution, relevance and value of others' ideas.

Points you may wish to consider:

- Do the ideas make new connections or open up new ways of viewing the subject? Have they informed or changed the way you think or feel about the subject area?

- How do they relate to the wider context (socio-political) or specific/local issues?

- Why is this knowledge useful or not? How does it inform your thinking or actions? What are the pros and cons, advantages but also the criticisms/limitations, for use in practice?

Examples of resources:

The College of Social Work; The Social Care Institute for Excellence (**www.scie.org.uk/**); local libraries.

CASE STUDY 7.2

Stage 2

Notes from Tony's work.

Recent research by Jones (2011) has indicated that personal effectiveness models, such as NLP, can become mechanisms of oppressive practice or disempowerment . . . All personal effectiveness tools, therefore, need to be used in a critical and ethical manner. As suggested by Alimo-Metcalfe and Alban-Metcalfe (2005), personal integrity is a crucial aspect here . . .

This means that effective application of NLP depends on my own motives and predisposition to ensure it is used positively rather than negatively. It is also only one set of ideas and therefore I need to combine this approach with relevant leadership approaches and techniques for enabling reflective practice and enhancing the team's learning culture . . . The recent Munro report (Munro 2011) shows the importance of such learning cultures . . .

The NLP literature specifically shows that language patterns and non-verbal communication are important to understand how good communication works. NLP theory has also been

---

useful in explaining some key elements of communication, and the link between thoughts, feelings and actions, as shown by Harris (2007) . . . The models provide a series of techniques for understanding and motivating people, i.e. working more effectively with them. For example, Smith (2006) shows how using inclusive instruction and embedded language such as 'we shall/we will have' as opposed to 'I want' increases the positivity and motivation of the statement . . .

The literature has informed a deeper understanding of certain negative responses made by staff to management proposals. It has also shown how initial reluctance and resistance to new ideas may be overcome, and this knowledge can be linked to wider communication/ motivation theory and to leadership approaches. For example, situational leadership as described by Hersey and Blanchard (1993) and Gray et al. (2010) provides inclusive approaches to . . . which can . . .

In addition, Goleman's (1998) work on emotional intelligence can assist in ensuring a more critical approach to . . .

Stage 3. Put the new knowledge and skills into practice – planning workplace activity.

Undertake a piece of work which involves a practical implementation/utilisation of this new learning, the new ideas and understanding, to develop an area of practice.

(a) Specify the rationale, aims and objectives for the utilisation of this learning in practice:

- Link to practice-based and organisational goals and outcomes.

- Link to original learning/CPD objectives.

(b) Develop an action plan which covers:

- What you will do, how and why.

- Alternatives and informed choices; explicitly and practically reason through your ideas (use the practical reasoning principles in Chapter 1).

- Ways to monitor and review progress and risk assessment – identify hazards, potential harm, control measures.

(c) Implement the plan and write up a critical analysis and evaluation of what happened:

- What happened and what affected the impact or end results?

- Were the objectives/intended outcomes achieved? How will any objectives that have not been met be addressed?

- How effectively were professional values integrated into the learning?

- Analyse feedback from key people involved or affected.

CASE STUDY **7.3**

Stage 3

Notes from Tony's work.

(i) The rationale, aims and objectives for the utilisation of this learning in practice:

Overall aims/purpose/rationale:

* *to enable the team to work together effectively to start seeking, collecting and recording service user feedback and meet organisational requirements*

* *develop my leadership and communication skills in relation to the above*

Objectives/desired outcomes:

* *communicate the policy effectively, be aware of and address anxieties and foster a team commitment to collecting service user feedback*

* *help plan for the right type of feedback to be collected which informs service delivery*

(ii) An action plan for this piece of work

Tasks:

* *Arrange a group supervision session*
  - *developing group understanding direction/cohesion/identity at this point outweighs potential disadvantages associated with group discussions (e.g. negative group dynamics) because . . .*
  - *group supervision can effectively incorporate the development of reflective practice which it turn can . . .*

* *Provide leadership and motivation in the team development session:*
  - *develop a situational leadership style . . .*
  - *review my own values and stance in regard to service user participation . . .*
  - *facilitate an empowering reflective discussion . . .*
  - *use relevant NLP techniques – Milton model; meta model; presuppositions*

* *Plan for what might happen, take account of 'risks':*
  - *The discussion may go off on a tangent; prompt critical feedback or disagreements; NLP techniques may be executed badly or unethically; staff may be upset or disengage*
  - *I therefore need to constantly monitor responses, non-verbal communication etc.*

(iii) Critical analysis and evaluation of the implementation and outcome of the action plan

Extract:

> *I was able to use some NLP techniques to build rapport with the team and to assist them in clearly defining both the desired objectives and the actions that needed to be undertaken to achieve them. Some NLP techniques worked very effectively – using the Milton model acknowledged the differing views and levels of motivation of people but also asserted that they have the resources to find a way forward. Overall, I felt I was able to establish the*

CASE STUDY **7.3** *(CONT.)*

beginnings of a learning culture here and a more developed understanding and commit-
ment to service user feedback and participation . . .

One member of staff, Pete (not his real name), was very suspicious and anxious about what
service user feedback would be used for and his input was forceful and disruptive, scaring the
other staff with tales of how the Social Work Task Force want service users to have the right to
'hire and fire' staff. This initially made me very annoyed and frustrated, and could potentially have
led to a conflict with him. By understanding the link between thoughts, feelings and actions, I
was more aware of what was happening to my responses (i.e. becoming aggressive) and I
consciously focused on a positive anchor, GSCC ethics for promoting service user views, with
which to challenge Pete in a non-threatening way . . . The discussion was then able to move on
but in future I can be even more aware of my reactions and avoid the initial aggressive tone.

I also asked specific questions of the group (the 'meta model') to try and move on from more
negative generalised positions, which were based on a range of anxieties around feeling at risk
of being individually criticised or the feedback being used to address perceived performance
issues. I directed our discussion to reflect on the differences between service user participation
and feedback, and why feedback should be sought, and how service users may feel services
should change, e.g. combining certain meetings. This discussion also allowed a more positive
perspective on the topic because it brought in our professional values and a collective
commitment to do the 'best job possible'. We were able to set a SMART objective – a 50 per
cent return rate of service user feedback forms over three months. We also set up a 'volunteer'
working party to redesign the feedback sheets, which we could see were not 'child-friendly'.

This is a longer-term project than initially envisaged and will require further similar sessions to
fully establish a working system and meet the objectives set above. The emergence of a team
learning culture could be seen, though, as the commitment to good practice overcame more
negative views, and a collective desire to do this 'properly' took hold, i.e. as an integral part
of practice and not as an add-on.

I didn't seek formal feedback at this stage but plan to collect this later on after three months
is up . . . details . . .; but a couple of positive comments as we left made me smile – 'that was
better than expected' and 'I quite enjoyed that'.

**Stage 4. Critically analyse and evaluate the impact and output of this on practice and on
service quality.**

**(4a) Identify the main impacts/changes/improvements for yourself as a practitioner (i.e.
your learning and personal/professional development; your thinking and behaviour;
your skill/expertise).**

Points you may wish to consider:

- What the impact/change/improvement was on your:
  - knowledge/understanding/ practice expertise;
  - self-managed learning abilities, attributes and skills;
  - professional role development/relationships/inter-professional working/accountability;

- links to relevant local/national professional frameworks and benchmarks, e.g. PCF domains/levels; codes of practice; management standards; frameworks; job descriptions;

- use of feedback from others involved in this work.

- What else do you now need to do to develop further?
  - ongoing learning/career/CPD needs; dissemination of learning to others; links to career progression/succession planning pathways/further feedback, e.g. 360-degree.

CASE STUDY 7.4

Stage 4a

Notes from Tony's work.

Examples of PCF areas developed:

Professionalism: emotional resilience . . .

Values and Ethics: ethical reasoning, person-centred approach, managing own values . . .

Professional Leadership: . . . addressing these key points:

• ensure individual and organisational practice is informed by current research and knowledge;

• promote a culture of professional curiosity.

My practical expertise has developed in this area of leadership and communication, in being able to investigate, research and use the NLP techniques effectively with groups and individuals whilst promoting a positive social work identity to service users and carers (see 4b).

I was able to adopt a situational leadership approach as detailed by Hersey and Blanchard (2007) . . . within group supervision in order to assist the team in exploring the issue of service user participation and in clearly defining the desired outcomes and actions needed to be undertaken . . . I was able to move an individual and others to a positive position in regard to the collection and use of service user feedback . . .

My learning has also developed in understanding how people think and react to spoken communication, also in the need to adopt a leadership approach that is responsive to a situation but which also works with people and empowers their underlying commitment to good practice, rather than impose things on them.

My leadership approach enacted good standards of management/leadership practice as shown by Skills for Care (SWRB, 2010), e.g. 'promote and meet service aims, objectives and goals', and 'value people, recognise and actively develop potential'. . . . I could have undertaken the group session in a way that simply told them what to do and bypassed the discussion and debate, i.e. undertaking an authoritarian style; or I could have used the NLP techniques unethically to manipulate people. But this would have been at odds with my own values and not fitted with my preferred leadership style . . . Undertaking the work in this way

---

CASE STUDY **7.4** *(CONT.)*

has confirmed the benefits and underlying importance of getting to understand the people you are working with, and of developing a team ownership of this initiative.

Undertaking the further reading in stage 2 as well as attending the initial workshops allowed me to 'digest' but also 'merge' the ideas and techniques with the aims of good leadership, supervision and reflective practice, developing new ideas to enhance and tailor the original learning for myself and this situation.

I can see that I worked around Kolb's (1984) experiential learning cycle – having the experience of the training workshops, reflecting on the material, using the reading to gather a range of ideas together and then establish a plan for the group session. Now I can move on again to further reflect and read more/attend further training if necessary, and plan for future experiences. I am aware that some of the NLP approaches were not natural to me and my skill level is still very basic. In the session I was dipping in and out of them and reverting to my usual style at times. At times using the meta model question 'how specifically?' seemed forced and repetitive. I need to read more and practise the techniques. I can also see how they can combine with my own techniques, e.g. 'cause and effect analysis', by using them in other situations.

I am also aware that I experienced some internal resistance to adopting this new approach of NLP and I prefer tried and tested routes. . . . For my future CPD this is something that needs to be addressed . . .

(4b) Identify the main impact/changes/improvements for professional and management practice, or operationally for a service.

Points you may wish to consider:

- Impact/change at organisational level – operation, performance, cost-benefit, development of a learning culture.

- Impact/change at stakeholder level, e.g. service users, their carers/families; partnerships.

- How performance improvement relates to the PCF, to current and national policy directives; national or local service quality standards or strategies.

- What was not achieved or had a negative impact: what else might be required to develop the practice or service further?

CASE STUDY 7.5

Stage 4b

Notes from Tony's work.

Examples of PCF areas developed:

Values and Ethics: enacting a person-centred approach . . .

Critical Reflection and Analysis: developing group supervision techniques

Professional Leadership: . . . addressing this key point:

• promote, articulate and support a positive social work identity.

My practical expertise has developed in this area of leadership, in being able to promote a positive social work identity to service users and carers by enabling a culture of respect for their feedback, and meaningful use of it that can enhance services.

1. *The longer term aim of Northshire to increase service user participation in a way that directly impacts on service delivery was obviously not completed within this session; however the team have a very clear method of how feedback will be obtained, with realistic timeframes to achieve this and ideas on how they can begin to seek feedback and participation in their day to day interactions with service users.*

   I also intend to explore how service user feedback can lead to a change in what is being provided, rather than just evaluate the effectiveness of what has been provided, i.e. to forward plan. The group supervision motivated my own commitment to making sure service user participation was undertaken in the most meaningful and 'proper' way. As an organisation we need to look at how we decide 'what is the right thing to do'. In NLP language we need to ensure we have a 'desired outcome' focused approach rather than a mechanistic problem-solving one in order to achieve better practice outcomes and service quality. I will undertake this using supervision discussions and research (e.g. further journal articles and use of SCIE 'best practice' sheets) . . .

2. *There are now measurable targets and outcomes – an agreed return rate of feedback forms within 3 months. The feedback sheet will also be revised to provide more meaningful and useful feedback which will help inform and develop service quality.*

3. *This should impact on service users in a positive way as their reactions, thoughts and ideas will be better represented . . .*

4. *The team's idea to use sub-headings in electronic case notes entitled 'service user feedback' will allow these records to be searched electronically and the data collected quickly and efficiently, providing an 'evidenced' chronology of feedback alongside an existing chronology of intervention.*

   This will improve usage for audit or quality purposes . . .

5. *This group supervision session supported directives within the Munro report (2011) and the recommendations of the Social Work Reform Board (2010).*

CASE STUDY 7.5 *(CONT.)*

These strengthen the importance of embedding and enabling learning within the work-place and although professional learning is the responsibility of all employees, managers have a special role to play . . .

6. *This group supervision session also supported Northshire's supervision policy to 'support and encourage reflective practice'. . .*

These case studies are rather detailed but aim to show a way that meaningful impact and output (measurable performance and more qualitative aspects) can be planned for and gained from work-based learning. Each individual stage could provide necessary evidence for CPD depending on what system is used and your overall purpose and objectives, such as appraisal, career progression or professional re-registration.

For further information, Appendix 4 provides an example of assessment criteria used to assess such learning as this at undergraduate level, which incorporate the Practical Reasoning Principles.

FURTHER READING

Day, M. (2002) *Assessment of Prior Learning: A Practitioner's Guide*. Cheltenham: Nelson Thornes.

Higgs, J., Richardson, B. and Dahlgren, M. (eds) (2004) *Developing Practice Knowledge for Health Professionals*. Edinburgh: Butterworth.

Martin, V. (2002) *Managing Projects in Health and Social Care*. London: Routledge.

Chapter 8
Writing up CPD

We have discussed the use and accreditation of CPD learning in academic environments and also shown one way that CPD evidence can be created from work-based learning using a specific example. This chapter takes this a step further to look at how you can develop an analytical style when writing up CPD and use the literature appropriately.

As we know, professional capability means approaching ideas and practice analytically, critically and evaluatively. It also requires the ability to articulate ideas coherently, usually in writing. Therefore any CPD output, such as a portfolio, should allow you to demonstrate and articulate your professional planning, reasoning, judgement and evaluation capabilities, the impact and outcome of your work in practice, as well as the ability to research, think and articulate ideas conceptually.

Writing can help determine how much change and development has occurred. It provides a structure and discipline, and by making the learning more permanent, it means it is not lost or forgotten. Research by Black and Plowright (2010) shows that reflective learning is perceived to be of better quality when thought through and written down, because this process helps review and deepen understanding. Thoughts look different when written down, and they become something different too, because the writing process is so dynamic. It allows ideas to evolve and connect with other thoughts; it encourages more discoveries to surface and improves construction of ideas. However, the potential to achieve this is dependent on writing ability, language and cultural issues, and whether the writing style required or adopted is aligned to the task.

Developing an analytical style

Overall, written work at a post-qualifying level, whether for formal programmes or not, requires the critical exploration, analysis and evaluation of your ideas and practice, as well as the ideas of others (e.g. as theory, research, policy, legislation). Essentially, this means going beyond descriptive writing, which cannot achieve the aims required for CPD. For example, a reflective narrative that takes a descriptive approach can easily become defensive in tone, with justifications for action that merely repeat arguments from theory or policy.

We can look at the key difference between descriptive and analytical writing. The difference is similar to that between a film (or a novel), and a documentary on the film or novel – the first just presents the story and the second gives you a particular view or 'take' on it. For example, *Pride and Prejudice* is essentially a love story between Elizabeth Bennet and Mr Darcy. A documentary, however, may take a view that the film missed many of the nuances of the book, or that the novel is a study of morality in nineteenth-century England. It then provides evidence for that view by using particular clips and other people's ideas, for example, and it will articulate that view using a series of explicit arguments and reasoned points. This is the main skill necessary for analytical and critical writing – being able to develop a view first and then a series of reasoned and evidenced points for it.

In other words, description only provides a straightforward or superficial 'story' which says what happened or what you or others did, and perhaps how and when it happened. Such description may be all that is necessary for certain situations, but I would expect that most professional circumstances would require more. Analytical writing, in contrast, focuses on taking a particular view first, formed by asking critical questions (e.g. why? so what? what else?) in order to gain insights, and by looking at deeper causes and implications. You will need to gain a distance and a perspective on your experience and learning (an objectivity), and you will need a variety of knowledge and understanding to do this. So, wider reading helps, because it provides a set of general concepts, ideas, models and theories to help inform your thinking. This approach scrutinises the original 'story' or event, analyses it and appraises it, but only summarises or uses the key bits that are relevant to the view taken on it. It then develops the additional commentary in order to make explicit and reasoned points that explain and critically support that view.

ACTIVITY 8.1

Moving from descriptive to analytical writing

Descriptive writing only tells us about things.

Example:

> I travelled here today by car and it took over 45 minutes, it usually only takes 30. I like driving because it is quicker than the bus, but it does get me really uptight though, especially at the amount of traffic, other inconsiderate road users, not to mention petrol prices . . .

Analytical writing has a view and critically discusses ideas in respect of this view, that is, it has a purpose.

Example:

> Travelling to work by car, although convenient, is expensive and also stressful and means I can arrive at work angry and bad-tempered. This can have a very negative effect on my colleagues . . .

Write your own example about a piece of learning you have been involved in using a descriptive style first. Then develop a view about that piece of learning (e.g. its effect on you) and rewrite your example so that this view is clear and makes an important point.

Try to use this approach for other pieces of writing where appropriate.

Working with the literature

In academic work you would probably also be expected to discuss and argue your points using a range of literature, which will take the form of references to theories, research, policies, legislation etc. This might also be productive for any type of CPD written output. We have seen the need for professionals to keep up-to-date with formal knowledge and be able to use it in a critical way in previous chapters.

Many people believe, though, that if someone else has already said something and managed to get it published, then they must be an expert and it must be true. This is not necessarily the case and, as we have already discussed, a professional view of knowledge expects to challenge it. Evidence from the literature will always be required to support any generalised assertions, ideas and opinions, but this can be achieved in a way that does not place an uncritical reliance on these ideas. Theory, in particular, can be used to answer some questions but also to pose others, rather than simply be regurgitated/repeated/quoted for its own sake; or to uncritically 'back up' practice or ideas.

Referencing the literature correctly is a skill in itself, and university libraries and support staff will have a range of material for guidance. The first requirement is to clarify your own ideas and viewpoint: start writing knowing what it is you want to say, as explained above. If you are not sure what your view is, then reflect further on your practice and read more in order to gain a better understanding and start to reach a view of your own. Once this is clear you can use the literature to help you discuss it in a series of critically reasoned points.

1. If you use direct quotes then 'pick out' the key words and critically extend the discussion with them and the ideas being presented, such as:

   > *It is very important that everyone involved in a process of improving service quality has a shared understanding of the issues and what is expected of them.*
   >
   > (Smith, 2002: 55)

   > *Sharing and understanding expectations are therefore key aspects to bear in mind when communicating with colleagues; however in practice this can prove troublesome if staff members are absent for crucial meetings.*

2. You can also paraphrase and then lead into a discussion, and start to support the point being made:

   > *It is essential that expectations are shared and understood by everyone involved in situations concerning service improvement (Smith, 2002). Communication strategies are therefore of major importance . . . however . . .*

   or

   > *A key aim with service quality development is clear communication and an exchange of information and ideas for staff, especially about roles and the type of activities they would be involved with. As Smith (2002) shows it is essential that expectations are shared and understood in such situations. However . . .*

ACTIVITY 8.2

Examples of integrating theory

(a) Why is this example doing it the wrong way?

> During the assessment (Middleton, 1997) I asked him a number of questions in order to ascertain his mental state and whether he was coping in the community.

(b) How does this next example start to get a debate going?

> Mental Health Services may have been sporadic over the years in terms of providing information, services, and working with service users and carers, but there appears to be more of an appreciation of the need to provide a more user friendly service (Harris, 2007). However, Neate (2008) would argue that the current Mental Health Bill and Mental Capacity Bill have very little input from service users and carers. This may potentially identify where the communication barrier stems from.

(c) How does this example show effective integration?

> It is fairly unusual for a GP to give a specific diagnosis in the early stages of illness. This can reflect a lack of adequate training for GPs, unwillingness to label somebody and issues of confidentiality of discussing a patient with their relatives (Carstairs *et al.*, 1990). However, in my own experience carers would often prefer a specific diagnosis, in terms of getting some understanding of the problems and in coming to terms with the long term implications, however bad the prognosis might be. Carers often feel excluded from these types of discussions but they can give the necessary information and empowerment (Wilkinson, 1998).

(a) Only notes the author and there is no hint to what is being referenced, i.e. what type of assessment it was that Middleton had written about.

(b) Uses words like 'but', 'however' and 'may' to start a discussion and link the ideas.

(c) The practice examples are reasoned through and then the theory helps explore or explain the ideas further or introduce them.

The skill of writing

Remember, writing is not a one-off activity, it is a process. Each draft will enable you to show areas of learning and development in more structured and explicit ways, as you build a better understanding of what you have done. Do not be afraid to keep going until you feel it is right. As stated at the beginning of the book, the self-managed learning associated with CPD requires an ability to evaluate and assess what we do against particular requirements or criteria, to recognise gaps and to persevere. This statement becomes very pertinent in regard to writing, I think! It can be hard, but when you express your learning and development coherently and articulate the progression you have made, it really is a great sense of personal achievement. It is a skill that will remain with you.

Good luck

I hope that your CPD experience has been facilitated by reading the discussions, following the guidance and undertaking the activities in this book. I wish you every success in your endeavour and trust that your CPD enhances your professional judgement, helps you develop further confidence in your role, and advances your career progression.

FURTHER READING

Cottrell, S. (2008) *The Study Skills Handbook*, 2nd edn. Basingstoke: Palgrave Macmillan.

Williams, K., Woolliams, M. and Spiro, J. (2012) *Reflective Writing: Pocket Study Skills.* Basingstoke: Palgrave Macmillan.

Rose, J. (2007) *The Mature Student's Guide to Writing.* Basingstoke: Palgrave Macmillan.

Appendix 1

Health and Care Professions Council: CPD standards and re-registration information

We define continuing professional development (CPD) as 'a range of learning activities through which health professionals maintain and develop throughout their career to ensure that they retain their capacity to practise safely, effectively and legally within their evolving scope of practice'. Put simply, CPD is the way professionals continue to learn and develop throughout their careers so they keep their skills and knowledge up to date and are able to work safely, legally and effectively.

Registrants must undertake CPD to stay registered with us. We have set CPD standards which say registrants must:

1. Maintain a continuous, up-to-date and accurate record of their CPD activities;

2. Demonstrate that their CPD activities are a mixture of learning activities relevant to current or future practice;

3. Seek to ensure that their CPD has contributed to the quality of their practice and service delivery;

4. Seek to ensure that their CPD benefits the service user; and

5. Upon request, present a written profile (which must be their own work and supported by evidence) explaining how they have met the standards for CPD.

Whenever a profession renews its registration, we randomly audit (check) the CPD of 2.5 per cent of professionals from that profession. Those registrants who are chosen for audit must submit a CPD profile to show how their CPD meets our standards.

There are links to a range of related documents on this site, e.g. CPD profile templates, profiles, examples of evidence, standards and guidance.

From: **www.hcpc-uk.org/registrants/cpd/index.asp**

Appendix 2
The NHS Leadership Framework

Leadership Framework overview

The Leadership Framework is comprised of seven domains. Within each domain there are four categories called elements and each of these elements is further divided into four descriptors. The website also provides a series of examples in practice, covering generic behaviours observed if an individual is not yet demonstrating this domain, and more specific examples where they are. These statements describe the leadership behaviours, which are underpinned by the relevant knowledge, skills and attributes which all staff should be able to demonstrate. Presented below is the basic detail; further information plus a series of downloadable documents are available via the website.

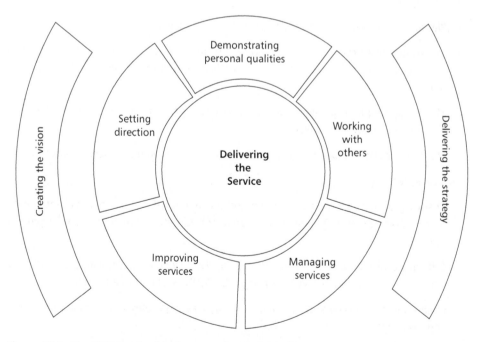

Figure A2.1 *The NHS Leadership Framework. Available from:* **www.leadershipacademy.nhs. uk/develop-your-leadership-skills/leadership-framework/the-framework-overview**

Leadership Framework: domains and elements

1. Demonstrating personal qualities

   - **Developing self-awareness** by being aware of own values, principles and assumptions, and by being able to learn from experiences.

   - **Managing yourself** by organising and managing self while taking account of the needs and priorities of others.

   - **Continuing personal development** by learning through participating in continuing professional development and from experience and feedback.

   - **Acting with integrity** by behaving in an open, honest and ethical manner.

2. Working with others

   - **Developing networks** by working in partnership with patients, carers, service users and their representatives, and colleagues within and across systems to deliver and improve services.

   - **Building and maintaining relationships** by listening, supporting others, gaining trust and showing understanding.

   - **Encouraging contribution** by creating an environment where others have the opportunity to contribute.

   - **Working within teams** to deliver and improve services.

3. Managing services

   - **Planning** by actively contributing to plans to achieve service goals.

   - **Managing resources** by knowing what resources are available and using personal influence to ensure that resources are used efficiently and safely, and reflect the diversity of needs.

   - **Managing people** by providing direction, reviewing performance, motivating others and promoting equality and diversity.

   - **Managing performance** by holding self and others accountable for service outcomes.

4. Improving services

   - **Ensuring patient safety** by assessing and managing risk to patients associated with service developments, balancing economic consideration with the need for patient safety.

   - **Critically evaluating** by being able to think analytically and conceptually, and to identify where services can be improved, working individually or as part of a team.

   - **Encouraging improvement** and innovation by creating a climate of continuous service improvement.

   - **Facilitating transformation** by actively contributing to change processes that lead to improving healthcare.

5. Setting direction

- **Identifying the contexts for change** by being aware of the range of factors to be taken into account.

- **Applying knowledge and evidence** by gathering information to produce an evidence-based challenge to systems and processes in order to identify opportunities for service improvements.

- **Making decisions** using personal values, and the evidence, to make good decisions.

- **Evaluating impact** by measuring and evaluating outcomes, taking corrective action where necessary and by being held to account for decisions.

6. Creating the vision

- **Developing the vision of the organisation**, looking to the future to determine the direction for the organisation.

- **Influencing the vision of the wider healthcare system** by working with partners across organisations.

- **Communicating the vision** and motivating others to work towards achieving it.

- **Embodying the vision** by behaving in ways which are consistent with the vision and values of the organisation.

7. Delivering the strategy

- **Framing the strategy** by identifying strategic options for the organisation and drawing upon a wide range of information, knowledge and experience.

- **Developing the strategy** by engaging with colleagues and key stakeholders.

- **Implementing the strategy** by organising, managing and assuming the risks of the organisation.

- **Embedding the strategy** by ensuring that strategic plans are achieved and sustained.

Available from: **www.leadershipacademy.nhs.uk/develop-your-leadership-skills/leadership-framework/the-framework-overview**

Appendix 3

Generic assessment descriptors for level 6 (bachelor's degree with honours)

Table A3.1 Generic assessment descriptors for level 6 (QAAHE, 2011)

Knowledge/ understanding	Learning/ development	Application of new knowledge/skills in practice	Critical, analytical, evaluative and communication skills
Systematic understanding of key aspects of the chosen field of study. Acquisition of coherent and detailed knowledge, informed by current literature. Ability to deploy accurately established techniques of analysis and enquiry. An appreciation of the uncertainty, ambiguity and limits of knowledge. Describe and comment upon particular aspects of current research.	Learning ability to undertake appropriate further training of a professional or equivalent nature. Ability to manage own learning. Exercise initiative and personal responsibility.	Frame appropriate questions to achieve a solution – or identify a range of solutions – to a problem. Apply the methods and techniques learned to review, consolidate, extend and apply knowledge and understanding, and to initiate and carry out projects. Decision-making in complex and unpredictable contexts.	Devise and sustain arguments and solve problems using appropriate ideas/techniques. Critically evaluate arguments, assumptions, abstract concepts and data (that may be incomplete), to make judgements. Communicate information, ideas, problems and solutions to both specialist and non-specialist audiences.

Taken from The UK Quality Code for Higher Education (QAAHE, 2011)

Appendix 4

Assessment grading criteria used to evaluate evidence of practice being developed within an academic CPD unit

Taken from: Bournemouth University (2011): *Unit Guide. Evidencing Professional/Management Learning (Work-based CPD).* Bournemouth: Bournemouth University.

Table A4.1 Example of CPD assessment grading criteria

	1. Systematic understanding of a body of knowledge gained as a result of professional or management learning.
Excellent evidence	Very thorough knowledge and understanding of the subject shown. Effective exploration of relevant and up-to-date sources. Highly developed conceptual understanding. Citations excellently presented with no errors.
Very good evidence	Thorough knowledge and understanding of the subject shown. Up-to-date and relevant sources. Sound conceptual understanding. Citations well presented with no errors.
Good evidence	Good level of knowledge and understanding of the subject shown. Up-to-date and mostly relevant sources. Some conceptual understanding of knowledge. Citations well presented with minor errors.
Some evidence	Relevant but limited knowledge shown. Some irrelevant sources. Limited conceptual understanding or much reproduced or described detail. Citations presented with some errors.
Not enough evidence	Misunderstanding or wrong/inappropriate knowledge shown. Irrelevant or not enough sources. Incorrect citations or major errors.

2. Evaluation of the impact of the learning on self as an autonomous and self-managed learner in a professional role.

Excellent evidence	Creative synthesis of this learning, e.g. with past, future. Own CPD is evaluated. Insightful and explicit understanding developed. Critical evaluation of changes/improvements.
Very good evidence	Learning and practice development is evaluated. Appreciation of other perspectives and use of feedback. Critical evaluation of changes/improvements.
Good evidence	Learning for self/practice is identified. Critical self-awareness and use of feedback. Clear evaluation of changes/improvements.
Some evidence	Limited identification of learning for self/practice. Some self-awareness evident. Limited awareness of changes/improvements.
Not enough evidence	Superficial identification of learning for self/practice. No self-awareness or use of feedback. No awareness of changes/improvements.

3. Application of new knowledge/skills in tackling and solving problems at a professional or management level.

Excellent evidence	Creative/original/insightful interpretations between learning, new knowledge/skills and practice. Seamless, critical integration of learning within a reasoning process. Exceptional ability to appreciate and take account of situational complexity and uncertainty in resulting decisions and actions. Ability to diagnose and apply appropriate and selected knowledge/skills/values to a practical situation to produce valid, creative/original solutions which are meaningful, effective and ethical.
Very good evidence	Critical interpretation of a range of learning, new knowledge/skills in and for practice. Shows a good flow and progression of ideas, with clearly made and justified points. Appreciation of situational complexity and uncertainty seen in developed deliberation and reasoning between goals and actions. Ability to diagnose and apply knowledge/skills/values to a practical situation to generate responses which are meaningful, effective and ethical, and offer some creativity or originality.
Good evidence	Some developed links between learning, new knowledge/skills and practice. Some flow or progression of ideas. Has points being made well with some justification.

Clear expression of situational goals with deliberated and reasoned links to action.

Reasonable sound ability to apply diagnostic skills to a practical situation to generate responses which are meaningful, effective and ethical. However, creativity and innovation may be absent.

Some evidence	Mechanistic application of learning, new knowledge/skills. Simple and limited connections.
	Tells us about a lot of things and makes a few clear points.
	Limited awareness of situational goals and links to action.
	There is limited ability to apply diagnostic and creative skills to a practical situation; or problem-solving ability limited to routine, mechanistic solutions.
Not enough evidence	No evidence of linkage between learning, new knowledge/skills and practice.
	No reasoning evident. Unclear. Confused. No awareness of or relationship between situational goals and resulting action.
	Problem-solving abilities not apparent.

---

4. Reflection on and critical evaluation of change/improvement in professional or management practice or in a service.

Excellent evidence	Comprehensive use of appropriate benchmarks to evidence improvement of practice/service.
	Critical evaluation of changes/improvements.
	Reflection resulting in new understanding/actions from the outcomes.
Very good evidence	Good use of appropriate benchmarks to evidence improvement of practice/service.
	Critical evaluation of changes/improvements.
	Reflection resulting in learning from the outcomes.
Good evidence	Clear use of appropriate benchmarks to evidence improvement of practice/service.
	Clear evaluation of changes/improvements.
	Reflection resulting in learning from the outcomes.
Some evidence	Some use of appropriate benchmarks to evidence improvement of practice/service.
	Limited awareness of changes/improvements.
	Reflection resulting in analysis of the outcomes.
Not enough evidence	No use of appropriate benchmarks to evidence improvement of practice/service.
	No awareness of changes/improvements.
	Descriptive reflection only.

References

Adams, R., Dominelli, L. and Payne, R. (2009) *Critical Practice in Social Work*, 2nd edn. Basingstoke: Palgrave Macmillan.

Argyris, C. and Schön, D. A. (1974) *Theory in Practice: Increasing Professional Effectiveness.* San Francisco: Jossey-Bass Publishers.

Atherton, J. S. (2011) *Doceo; Competence, Proficiency and Beyond* [Online: UK]. Available from: www.doceo.co.uk/background/expertise.htm

Baxter Magolda, M. (1996) Epistemological development in graduate and professional education. *Review of Higher Education*, 19 (3), 283–304.

Beckett, D. and Hager, P. (2002) *Life, Work and Learning: Practice in Postmodernity.* London: Routledge.

Beddoe, L. (2009) Creating continuous conversation: Social workers and learning organisations. *Social Work Education: The International Journal*, 28 (7), 722–36.

Beverley, A. and Worsley, A. (2007) *Learning and Teaching in Social Work Practice.* London: Palgrave Macmillan

Biggs, J. (2007) *Teaching for Quality Learning at University.* Buckingham: SHRE and OU.

Black, P. E. and Plowright, D. (2010) A multi-dimensional model of reflective learning for professional development. *Reflective Practice*, 11 (2), 245–58.

Blewett, J. (2011) Continuing professional development: Enhancing high-quality practice. *In:* Seden, J., Matthews, S., McCormick, M. and Morgan, A. (eds) *Professional Development in Social Work*. London: Routledge, 185–91.

Boshuizen, H. P. A., Bromme, R. and Gruber, H. (eds) (2004) *Professional Learning: Gaps and Transitions on the Way from Novice to Expert.* Dordrecht, the Netherlands: Kluwer Academic Publishers.

Bourner, T. (2003) Assessing reflective learning. *Education and Training*, 45 (5), 267.

Bradbury, H., Frost, N., Kilminster, S. and Zukas, M. (eds) (2010) *Beyond Reflective Practice: New Approaches to Professional Lifelong Learning.* London: Routledge.

Brockbank, A. and McGill, I. (2002) *Facilitating Reflective Learning through Mentoring and Coaching.* Kogan Page: London.

Brookfield, S. (1987) *Developing Critical Thinkers.* Milton Keynes: Open University Press.

Brown, K., Rutter, L., Keen, S. and Rosenorn-Lanng, E. (2012) *Partnerships, Continuing Professional Development (CPD) and the Accreditation of Prior Learning (APL).* Birmingham: Learn to Care.

Burton and Jackson (2006) Work-based learning. *In:* Jones, R. and Jenkins, F. (eds) *Developing the Allied Health Professional.* Oxford: Radcliffe Publishing, 65–75.

Cleary, P., Whittaker, R., Gallacher, J., Merrill, B., Jokinen, L., Carette, M. and members of the Centre for Social and Educational Research Team (University of Barcelona) (2002) *Social Inclusion through APEL: The Learners' Perspective. Comparative Report.* Centre for Research in Lifelong Learning, Glasgow Caledonian University, Glasgow. Available from: http://crll.gcal.ac.uk/SOCRATESSite/home.html

Clegg, S. (2009) Forms of knowing and academic development practice. *Studies in Higher Education,* 34 (4), 403–16.

Coffield, F., Moseley, D., Hall, E. and Ecclestone, K. (2004) *Learning Styles and Pedagogy in post-16 Learning: A Systematic and Critical Review.* London: Learning Skills Research Centre (now LSN).

Collins, E. and Daly, E. (2011) *Decision-Making and Social Work in Scotland: The Role of Evidence and Practice Wisdom.* Glasgow: Institute for Research and Innovation in Social Services (IRISS).

Cooper, B. (2008) Continuing professional development: A critical approach. *In:* Fraser, S. and Matthews, S. (eds) *The Critical Practitioner in Social Work and Health Care.* London: Sage, 222–37.

Cooper, B. (2011) Careering through social work: Metaphors of continuing professional devleopment. *In:* Seden, J., Matthews, S., McCormick, M. and Morgan, A. (eds) *Professional Development in Social Work.* London: Routledge, 178–84.

Cox, E. and Green, V. (2001) *Embedding APEL: Encouraging APEL Provision in Continuing Education.* Oxford: Oxford Brookes University. Available from: www.escalate.ac.uk/resources/apel

Davis, R., Gordon, J. and Walker, G. (2011) Learning in practice: Some reflections on the student's journey. *In:* Seden, J., Matthews, S., McCormick, M. and Morgan, A. (eds) *Professional Development in Social Work.* London: Routledge, 143–9.

Doel, M., Nelson, P. and Flynn, E. (2008) Experiences of post-qualifying study in social work. *Social Work Education,* 27 (5), 549–71.

Dreyfus, H. L. and Dreyfus, S.E. (1986) *Mind over Machine: The Power of Human Intuition and Expertise in the Age of the Computer.* Oxford: Basil Blackwell.

Dunne, J. (2011) 'Professional wisdom' in 'practice'. *In:* Bondi, L., Carr, D., Clark, C. and Clegg, C. (eds) *Towards Professional Wisdom: Practical Deliberation in the People Professions.* Farnham: Ashgate, 13–26.

Eraut, M. (1985) Knowledge creation and knowledge use in professional contexts. *Studies in Higher Education,* 10 (2), 117–33.

Eraut, M. (1994) *Developing Professional Knowledge and Competence.* London: Routledge

Fenstermacher, G. (1994) The knower and the known: The nature of knowledge in research on teaching. *Review of Research in Education,* 20 (1), 3–56.

Fook, J., Ryan, M. and Hawkins, L. (2000) *Professional Expertise: Practice, Theory and Education for Working in Uncertainty.* London: Whiting and Birch Ltd.

Golding, C. (2011) Educating for critical thinking: Thought-encouraging questions in a community of inquiry. *Higher Education Research and Development,* 30 (3), 357–70.

Gordon, J., Cooper, B. and Dumbleton, S. (2009) *How Do Social Workers Use Evidence in Practice? Final Report.* (34): Practice-based Professional Learning Centre.

Gray, D. (2007) Facilitating management learning: Developing critical reflection through reflective tools. *Management Learning,* 38 (5), 495–513.

Gray, I., Parker, J., Rutter, L. and Williams, S. (2010) Developing communities of practice: Effective leadership, management and supervision in social work. *Social Work and Social Sciences Review,* 14 (2), 20–36.

Guile, D. and Young, M. (1996) Further professional development and further education teachers: Setting a new agenda for work-based learning. *In:* Woodward, I. (ed) *Continuing Professional Development: Issues in Design and Delivery.* London: Cassell.

Hafford-Letchfield, T., Leonard, K., Begum, N. and Chick, N. (2008) *Leadership and Management in Social Care.* London: Sage.

HEPI (Higher Education Policy Institute) (2004) *Credit Accumulation and Transfer, and the Bologna Process.* Bahram Bekhradnia: HEPI.

Hock, D. (2000) The Art of Chaordic Leadership. Leader to Leader, No. 15. The Peter F. Drucker Foundation for Nonprofit Management. Available from: www.pfdf.org/leaderbooks/L2L/winter2000/hock.html.

Howe, D. (2002) Relating theory to practice. *In:* Davis, M. (ed) *Blackwell Companion to Social Work.* Oxford: Blackwell, 81–7.

Honey, P. and Mumford, A. (1982) *Manual of Learning Styles.* Maidenhead: Peter Honey.

Jarvis, P. (1992) Quality in practice: The role of education. *Nurse Education Today,* 21 (1), 3–10.

Ikuenobe, P. (2001) Questioning as an epistemic process of critical thinking. *Educational Philosophy and Theory, 33* (3 & 4), 325–41.

Johnson, B. and Walsh, A. (2005) *SEEC companion to the QAA Guidelines on the Accreditation of Prior Learning.* London: SEEC.

Jones, S. and Joss, S. (1995) Models of professionalism. *In:* Yelloly, M. and Henkel, M. (eds) *Learning and Teaching in Social Work.* London: Jessica Kingsley Publishers, 15–31.

Keen, S., Brown, K., Parker, J., Gray, I. and Galpin, D. (eds) (2012) *Newly Qualified Social Workers: A Practice Guide to the Assessed and Supported Year in Employment,* 2nd edn. London: Sage.

Kemmis, S. (1985) Action research and the politics of reflection. *In: Reflection: Turning Experience into Learning.* London: Kogan Page, 139–64.

Knowles, M. (1980) *The Modern Practice of Adult Education. From Pedagogy to Andragogy,* 2nd edn. Englewood Cliffs: Prentice Hall/Cambridge.

Kolb, D. A. (1984) *Experiential Learning: Experience as the Source of Learning and Development.* New Jersey: Prentice Hall.

Kondrat, M. E. (1992) Reclaiming the practical: Formal and substantive rationality in social work practice. *Social Service Review,* 66 (2), 237–55.

Kundin, D. M. (2010) A conceptual framework for how evaluators make everyday practice decisions. *American Journal of Evaluation,* 31 (3), 347–62.

Laming, L. (2003) *The Victoria Climbié Inquiry Report of an Inquiry by Lord Laming.* London: The Stationery Office.

Laming, L. (2009) *The Protection of Children in England: A Progress Report.* Norwich: The Stationery Office.

Lave, J. and Wenger, E. (1991) *Situated Learning: Legitimate Peripheral Participation.* Cambridge: Cambridge University Press.

Lonergan B. (1992) *Insight: A Study of Human Understanding.* Toronto: University of Toronto Press.

Lucas, J. R. (1994) The lay-out of arguments. *In:* Krawietz, W., MacCormick, N. and Von Wright, G. H. (eds) *Prescriptive Formality and Normative Rationality in Modern Legal Systems.* Berlin: Robert S. Summers.

McArdle, K. and Coutts, N. (2010) Taking teachers' continuing professional development (CPD) beyond reflection: Adding shared sense-making and collaborative engagement for professional renewal. *Studies in Continuing Education,* 32 (3), 201–15.

Marton, F. and Säljö, R. (1976) On qualitative differences in learning: 1. Outcome and process. *British Journal of Educational Psychology,* 46, 4–11.

Mathews, I. and Crawford, K. (2011) *Evidence-Based Practice in Social Work.* Exeter: Learning Matters.

Mingers, J. (2000) What is it to be critical? Teaching a critical approach to management undergraduates. *Management Learning,* 31 (2), 219–37.

Munro, E. (2008) Improving reasoning in supervision. *Social Work Now,* 40 (August), 3–10.

Munro, E. (2011) *The Munro Review of Child Protection: Final Report. A Child-Centred System.* (CM 8062). Norwich: The Stationery Office.

Noble, C. (2001) Researching field practice in social work education: Integration of theory and practice through the use of narratives. *Journal of Social Work,* 1 (3), 347–60.

Oko, J. (2011) *Understanding and Using Theory in Social Work,* 2nd edn. Exeter: Learning Matters.

O'Sullivan, J. (2006) Continuing professional development. *In:* Jones, R. and Jenkins, F. (eds) *Developing the Allied Health Professional.* Oxford: Radcliffe Publishing, 1–20.

O'Sullivan, T. (2011) *Decision Making in Social Work,* 2nd edn. Basingstoke: Palgrave Macmillan.

Otienoh, R.O. (2011) Teacher's lack of deeper analytical reflections: Who is to blame? *Reflective Practice,* 12 (6), 733–47.

Potter, C. and East, J. F. (2000) Developing reflective judgement through MSW education. *Journal of Teaching in Social Work,* 20 (1/2), 217–37.

Prosser, M. and Trigwell, K. (1999) *Understanding Learning and Teaching: The Experience in Higher Education.* Buckingham: Society for Research in Higher Education and Open University Press.

QAAHE (2004) *Guidelines on the Accreditation of Prior Learning.* Mansfield: QAAHE.

QAAHE (2008) *The Framework for Higher Education Qualifications in England, Wales and Northern Ireland.* Gloucester: Quality Assurance Agency for Higher Education.

QAAHE (2011) *UK Quality Code for Higher Education Part A: Setting and Maintaining Threshold Academic Standards. Chapter A1: The National Level.* Gloucester: Quality Assurance Agency for Higher Education.

Race, P. (2010) *Making Learning Happen,* 2nd edn. London: Sage

Rutter, L. (2012) *Professional Education and Personal Epistemology: A Post Qualifying Social Work Case Study. D Prof Thesis.* Bournemouth: Bournemouth University.

Rutter, L. and Brown, K. (2011) *Critical Thinking and Professional Judgement for Social Work*, 3rd edn. London: Sage/Learning Matters.

Ropo, E. (2004) Teaching expertise. *In:* Boshuizen, H. P. A., Bromme, R. and Gruber, H. (eds) *Professional Learning: Gaps and Transitions on the Way from Novice to Expert.* Dordrecht, the Netherlands: Kluwer Academic Publishers, 159–79.

Säljö, R. (1979) *Learning in the Learner's Perspective: 1: Some Commonplace Misconceptions.* Reports from the Institute of Education, University of Gothenburg, 76.

Schön, D. A. (2001) The crisis of professional knowledge and the pursuit of an epistemology of practice. *In:* Raven, J. and Stephenson, J. (eds) *Competence in the Learning Society.* New York: Peter Lang, 185–207.

Seden, J., Matthews, S., McCormick, M. and Morgan, A. (eds) (2011) *Professional Development in Social Work.* London: Routledge.

Seden, J. and McCormick, M. (2011) Caring for yourself, being managed and professional development. *In:* Seden, J., Matthews, S., McCormick, M. and Morgan, A. (eds) *Professional Development in Social Work.* London: Routledge, 171–7.

Senge, P. (1990). *The Fifth Discipline: The Art and Practice of the Learning Organisation.* London: Century Business.

Simons, P. R-J. and Ruijters, M. C. P. (2001) Learning professionals: Towards an integrated model. *In:* Boshuizen, H. P. A., Bromme, P. and Gruber, H. (eds) *Professional Learning Gaps and Transitions on the Way from Novice to Expert.* Dordrecht: Kluwer.

Smith, M. K. (2001) *David A. Kolb on Experiential Learning.* The Encyclopedia of Informal Education. [Online] Available from: www.infed.org/b-explrn.htm

Strampel, K. and Oliver, R. (2010) They think they are learning, but are they? Strategies for implementing Web 2.0 to positively impact student learning. *In:* Steel, C. H., Keppell, M. J., Gerbic, P. and Housego, S. (eds) *Curriculum, Technology and Transformation for an Unknown Future.* Proceedings ASCILITE Sydney 2010, 924–35

Streumer, B. (2009) Practical reasoning. *In:* O'Connor, T. and Sandis, C. (eds) *The Blackwell Companion to the Philosophy of Action.* Oxford: Blackwell.

SWRB (2010) *Building a Safe and Confident Future: One Year On.* London: Social Work Reform Board. Available from: www.education.gov.uk/swrb

SWRB (2011) *Proposals for Implementing a Coherent and Effective National Framework for the Continuing Professional Development of Social Workers.* London: Social Work Reform Board. Available from: www.education.gov.uk/swrb

SWTF (2009) *Building a Safe, Confident Future. The Final Report of the Social Work Task Force: November 2009.* London: Social Work Task Force.

Taylor, C. and White, S. (2000) *Practising Reflexivity in Health and Welfare: Making Knowledge.* Buckingham: Open University Press.

Taylor, C. and White, S. (2001) Knowledge, truth and reflexivity: The problem of judgement in social work. *Journal of Social Work,* 1 (1), 37–58.

TCSW (2012) *Understanding What Is Meant by Holistic Assessment*: ASYE 1 (Version 1). May 2012. The College of Social Work. Available from: www.collegeofsocialwork.org/uploadedFiles/TheCollege/CollegeLibrary/Reform_resources/holistic-assessmentASYE1.pdf

Thompson, N. and Pascal, J. (2012) Developing critically reflective practice. *Reflective Practice: International and Multidisciplinary Perspectives,* 13 (2), 311–25.

Thompson, S. and Thompson, N. (2008) *The Critically Reflective Practitioner*. Basingstoke: Palgrave Macmillan.

Tynjala, P., Valimaa, J. and Sarja, A. (2003) Pedagogical perspectives on the relationship between higher education and working life. *Higher Education,* 46, 147–66.

Tyreman, S. (2000) Promoting critical thinking in health care: Phronesis and criticality. *Medicine, Health Care and Philosophy,* 3, 117–24.

Usher, R. and Bryant, I. (1989) *Adult Education as Theory, Practice and Research: The Captive Triangle*. London: Routledge.

Walker, J., Crawford, K. and Parker, J. (2008) *Practice Education in Social Work: A Handbook for Practice Teachers, Assessors and Educators*. Exeter: Learning Matters.

White, S. (2009) Fabled uncertainty in social work. *Journal of Social Work,* 9 (2), 222–35.

Wick, C., Pollock, R. and Jefferson, A. (2010) *The Six Disciplines of Breakthrough Learning: How to Turn Training and Development into Business Results*, 2nd edn. London: John Wiley and Sons.

Williams, S. and Rutter, L. (2010) *The Practice Educator's Handbook*. Exeter: Learning Matters.

Williams, S., Rutter, L. and Gray, I. (2012) *Promoting Individual and Organisational Learning in Social Work*. London: Sage/Learning Matters.

Woodward, I. (ed) (1996) *Continuing Professional Development: Issues in Design and Delivery*. London: Cassell.

Index